Heart-To-Heart
Talks with God

Kathy Fleiger

ISBN 978-1-64559-951-7 (Paperback)
ISBN 978-1-64559-952-4 (Digital)

Covenant Books, Inc.
11661 Hwy 707
Murrells Inlet, SC 29576
www.covenantbooks.com

CONTENTS

Introduction...11

Section 1:   Almighty God, Our Father
             Our God 15
             God Is Here and Now 17
             The Word of God Is a Light 19
             God Our Supplier of Our Every Need 21
             The Sun—the Son..23
             Power in God's Word...25
             God's Power through Water 27
             Power of God's Blessing 29
             Mercy..31
             Grace...33
             Light of God...35
             Kingdom of God 37
             No Luck 39
             Bought with a Price 41
             God Is for Us..43
             Shadows 45
             God Comes into the World 47
             Give Me Jesus..49
             Water...51

Knocking Down Barriers 53

Dust and Ash...55

Our Refuge...57

Advertisement Campaigns 58

Mend and Restore 60

God Reveals Himself 62

Open Arms..64

Mysteries of God 66

I Am..68

Timeless 70

Angels..72

My Rock..74

One God 76

God Lights the Way.....................................78

Giving Good Things.....................................80

Camouflage 82

Always Ready...84

One True God 86

Section 2:   The Boundless Love of God

God Is Love..89

Power of God's Love 91

Power in God's Promises...............................92

Generosity of God.......................................94

Christmas 96

Christ Is the Same 98

It's Easter, But..100

Touch 102

Blessing 104

Reflections..106

God's Steadfastness 108

Clouds 110

Broken yet Loved 112

Real Life 114

Love of God 115

Our Identity 117

Trinity 119

Peace 120

A Bible 122

Dirty Laundry 123

Why Trust in the Lord? 125

God Is Always with Us 127

God Reigns in Love 129

Amazing Love of God 131

Abundant Life with God 133

Gifts of God 135

Good Gifts from God 137

God Is the Answer 139

Home 141

Poor 143

Our Very Present Help 145

God Carries and Sustains Us 147

Remember 149

Selflessness 151

God's Word Is Truth 153

God's Love Empowers Us 155

Our Loving God 157

Section 3:   God Speaks to His Children

God Speaks to Our Heart, Our Soul, Our Mind 161

Busy 163

Disciples 165

Run the Race 167

Patience 169

Power of the Holy Spirit 171

God's Power to Change Us 173

Power in God's Truths........................... 175

Being Imitators.................................... 177

The Tongue 179

Ears to Hear 181

It Is Never Too Late.............................. 183

Making Decisions.................................. 185

Followers of Christ 187

Do Not Fear, Only Believe...................... 189

Fear 191

Fire.. 193

Ready 195

Kindness.. 197

Gentleness 199

Goodness.. 201

Self-Control.. 203

Joy... 205

Never Give Up...................................... 207

Encourage One Another 209

Heart.. 211

Sharing.. 213

Prayer 215

Affliction 217

Open and Close Doors 219

Recipe for Life 221

Return to the Lord................................ 223

Idleness... 225

Junctions: Which Way to Go.................................227

Clutter and Burdens 229

Wonders 231

God Speaks the Truth 233

Section 4:   Living Our Life for Christ

Live in and for Christ 237

A Tree 239

Love Is Patient 241

Walking with God.................................243

Who Is Counting on Who? 244

Live for Christ 246

Workers in the Kingdom of God 248

Power of God Working In One Life.................................250

Power of God's Path.................................251

Doers of the Word 253

Pine Cones 255

Living in Christ 257

Live in Hope.................................259

Lamenting.................................261

Windmills 263

Church Sign 265

Equipped.................................267

Choose 269

Struggles.................................271

Spiritual Strength.................................273

Storage.................................275

The Greatest.................................277

The Way.................................279

Tumbleweed 281

People Watching.................................283

DIY, Do It Yourself...285

Trusting in God..287

Challenges..289

Deceiving Ourselves 291

Power on Our Knees...293

Wisdom...295

Thoughts..297

Step Aside..299

Desires, Craving, and Longings 301

Abide in Christ...303

Never Alone or on Our Own................................305

Christ the Center of our Life 307

Section 5:   Growing in Faith and in Christ

Grow, Develop, and Shine in Christ 311

A Song...313

Action while Waiting..315

Expectations 317

Power of God through Us...................................319

Flashlights 321

Living in God's Love...323

Living in God's Forgiveness 325

Worthy of Praise...327

Focus...329

Harvesting..331

Never Flag in Zeal 333

Face of Jesus..335

Grow Where You Are Planted..............................337

Lighthouse..339

Gravity 340

New Every Morning...342

Eye on the Ball..344

Daylight Savings Time...346

Northern Lights..348

Aha Moments with God......................................350

Fishing..352

Glisten, Sparkle, Shine..354

Honor and Glory to God 356

Arise, Go 358

Giving of Ourselves 360

Give Thanks 362

Chores and Responsibilities 364

Cling to Jesus...366

Character..368

Endure 370

Thanks Be to God 372

Flourish with Jesus...373

Blind, but Now I See 375

Convenient or Commitment 377

Faith in Action...379

Grow in God's Grace and Love 381

INTRODUCTION

Grace, mercy and peace will be with us, from
God the Father and from Jesus Christ the Father's
Son, in truth and love. (2 John 1:3)

Let the words of my mouth and the meditation
of my heart be acceptable in thy sight, O Lord,
my rock and my redeemer. (Psalm 19:14)

God loves each one of us with His unconditional, everlasting, and
steadfast love. We are so important to Him that He wants a relationship with each one of us. That relationship begins when we believe
and trust in Him, and it continues to grow throughout our life.

As our faith and trust in Him grow, we become aware and sensitive to His love and His ability to speak to our heart, mind, and soul.
He speaks to each of us about a variety of things and messages that
deal with His love for us, being our Savior and Lord, our life in Him,
our world, our family, our attitude and behavior, about His word and
promises, and about our life with Him and so much more.

As followers of Christ, Christ is the center and focus of our
lives. It is only possible to put Christ first with His help and daily
recommitment to Him. So often we take Him and His word for
granted. We ignore Him and go on our own way by doing what we
think is okay and right. But when life gets messy, confusing, or to
heavy, we finally call upon Him to rescue us. Jesus wants to be the

center of our life all the time, not just when we need help or are desperate. He wants us to love Him, talk to Him, listen to Him, and walk with Him all the time.

When Jesus is the center of our being, many things take on new life and become significant and meaningful because of Jesus. Jesus helps us to see things in a new light. He helps us put a new focus, a new emphasis on things, objects, and concepts in our life. A rock, a tree, a bush, water, clouds, sharing, patience, or fire take on new meanings in and with Jesus. When we see or hear about these object and concepts, it becomes a way for us to remember Jesus's truths and teachings. Jesus breaks into our world and speaks to our heart, mind, and soul.

As God reveals more of Himself, His love, and insights, we learn and grow in faith. He blesses us with moments, thoughts, talks, messages, and insights about Himself, His love, and His world. This hopefully drives us back to the scripture, to study and learn more about Him, His word, and promises. And since everything we have is from God, let us be more thoughtful, caring, and loving toward everyone and everything in this world because of Jesus.

The Lord is good, and His steadfast love endures forever. May you be blessed by these messages, talks, prayers, and meditations to be a blessing to others.

SECTION 1

Almighty God, Our Father

Our God

Our God is a God of love, grace, mercy, and forgiveness. He is a God of power and might. A God that provides all things for His children. A God that not only is all-powerful, all-present, and all-knowing, but also is our Heavenly Father.

If you want to know God, then you must get to know His Son, Jesus. If you know Jesus Christ, the Son of God, then you know God. God shows and reveals to us who He is through His Son, Jesus.

In the Bible, Jesus heals the leper and Lazarus and the afflictions of people, in His way and in His time. He gives joy and peace to Paul while He was in prison, as well through our trials. Jesus breaks down barriers between cultures and religions, between Gentiles and Jews, and between friends and enemies. He dispels fear and worry to the disciples and gives calmness and peace to those in fear and even to those who fear flying.

Jesus, our Savior and Lord, is the foundation of our salvation then and now. He is the solid rock on which we stand and build our church. Jesus shows love to sinners and the righteous. Jesus is our friend and cares for all.

Jesus is always there for us, even when we stray, get lost, or neglect Him. Even when we get caught up in our own selfishness and worldliness, Jesus is still there for each of us.

He is always seeking and calling the lost to return to Him. He loves us so much He never turns away or leaves us. His steadfast love endures forever, and He even loves us when we were sinners.

He alone is God, the great I Am. He is the alpha and the omega, the beginning and the end. He is our everlasting Father and Prince of Peace. He loves us so much, He sends His only Son, Jesus, to die on the cross and for our salvation. He is our refuge, our light and truth, our deliverer, our healer, our strength, our comforter, our protector and guard, and our way to living water and everlasting life. He takes care of us and loves us when we stumble and fall. He equips us for our journey here on earth. He is this and so much more. We can only know in part of all that He is, but the more we listen, learn, change, and grow in faith and knowledge, the more God shows and reveals to us.

Our God is steadfast and everlasting.

May these meditations, talks, and moments be a blessing to you.

GOD IS HERE AND NOW

The summer is filled with sun, swimming, boating, golfing, reading, camping, fishing, evenings spent outside, and sports events. So many things to do as we try and get it all done before fall comes. We get very busy and forget to take God with us. But God is always with us and waiting for us to include him in all our activities and to trust him in all areas of our life.

God is with us and in the here and now. Many things during the summer remind us of God, especially the forest, the stars, and the lakes and ocean. Even the sun, sunscreen, and water remind us of God.

The *sun* shines for many days during the summer. John 8:11 says that "God is the Light of the world and he who follows me will not walk in darkness but will have the Light of Life." Next time you are out enjoying the sunshine, thank God for His promises and for being the light of the world.

Sunscreen is necessary when living in a sunshine state. Ephesians 6:11 says that we "need to put on the whole armor of God that we may be able to stand against the wiles of the devil." God provides us with a shield and a refuge when daily struggles and hurt comes our way. The next time you put on sunscreen on your child or yourself, pray and ask God for His protection.

Water is always a component for summertime. John 3:5 declares "that truly I say to you unless one is born of water and of the spirit he cannot enter the kingdom of heaven." The next time you are swimming or enjoying the coolness of the lake or enjoying a glass of water, remember and thank God for the baptismal waters of Christ, which gives us forgiveness, peace, healing, and eternal life.

Summer is truly a time that reminds us of God, and it is a time to reflect on God's gifts and promises to each of us. He gives us everyday items to see and remember so we do not forget Him or His word. Summer is a time of renewal, recreation, healing, restoration, growth, and rediscovery of the love and power of God.

God's love abides and dwells in his people. His love motivates us to change, to live in and for Him. His power and wisdom is also *here* and *now*. Take him with you wherever you go and whatever you do. God gives us strength to change and to live in His forgiveness, love, peace, and joy. *He* is and will complete the good work and the plan He has begun in you.

Let us trust God and let Him work within each of us and through us. God is *here* and *now*.

Thanks be to God. Amen.

THE WORD OF GOD
IS A LIGHT

Thy word is a lamp to my feet and a light to my path. (Psalm 119:105)

You are the light of the world. A city set on a hill cannot be hid, Nor do men light a lamp and put is under a bushel, but on a stand, and it gives light to all the house. Let your light so shine before men, that they may see your good works and give glory to your Father who is in heaven. (Matthew 5:14–16)

Jesus spoke to them, saying, I am the light of the world, he who follows me will not walk in darkness, but will have the light of life. (John 8:12)

There is a TV commercial for Motel 6. The guy says, "We'll leave the light on for you."

God is light. God leaves the light on for us.

God directs and guides us on the right path. He knows the path is not easy, so He leaves the light on so we can see and follow Him.

As followers of God, we too become God's light in this world. So we keep our light from God burning by fueling it. A flame will burn out if it is not fed. Our source of fuel is Christ, the true light.

He continues to guide and direct each of us for our ministry and service. Spending time with Christ, in prayer and worship, allows us to be renewed, strengthened, and reenergized, which are essential to keep our lights burning and shining.

We must avoid falling into a lifestyle that is uncharacteristic of Christ. We must constantly keep watch of our thoughts, activities, and daily routines so they don't take our focus off Christ and His ministry. We give Jesus our worries, frustrations, disappointments, and wants so they do not overwhelm or overtake us and quench the light within us.

God's light is on for you and me.

God's light shines for us to see. His path is shining and showing us His way, to an everlasting life. God restores, renews, and fills us with the Holy Spirit to encourage and empower us for our journey. Let us keep our focus on Him, His way, His love, His life, and His light. As we focus on Christ, we become His light and encouragement to a world in need.

The word of God is light for you and me and the world.

Thanks be to God. Amen.

GOD OUR SUPPLIER OF OUR EVERY NEED

Behold, God is my salvation; I will trust, and will not be afraid; for the Lord God is my strength and my song and he has become my salvation. (Isaiah 12:2)

And my God will supply every need of yours according to his riches in glory in Christ Jesus. (Philippians 4:19)

We live in a world of uncertainty. We don't know what the countries of the world will do to other countries, the financial world is always up and down, and nothing seems to be stable for any length of time. In and amongst the uncertainty and instability, God is still God and in control. The God of Abraham and Jacob is with us. He gives us life, love, and hope. He provides stability, love, and hope in Him through faith. In times of need, we turn to God, we reach out, and we ask for His help. We ask Him to walk with us and hold on to us. We ask for His help to live in faith and in His grace and promises. We ask Him to help us balance our desires with our true needs. And we thank and praise Him for being our comforter, refuge, and provider in times of turmoil.

God truly is the supplier of our every need. We trust and believe in His strength and might to provide for us, according to His steadfast love and mercy.

Lord, help us look to You for strength, wealth, abundance, true needs, our financial stability, and grace. You provide the children of Israel with food in the desert. You feed the multitudes with five loaves and two fish. So by Your grace, our cup overflows, and there is plenty for all. Help us loosen our grip on what You give us and help us to trust solely in You and Your love. You supply our every need. You give us love and life. We become safe and secure—in You alone. Lord, move us from fear to love and bless us with Your treasures, Your spirit, and Your peace.

Thanks be to God.

Amen.

THE SUN—THE SON

The *sun* is shining today. It is finally warm outside. Summer is here.

The sun gives off heat and light that the earth needs to support life. Without the sun, the earth could not support life. It is also the center of our solar system and holds it together. If the sun were any different to how it is, life on the earth would not exist. It is the perfect size, age, distance/place, temperature, and brightness for life to exist on earth. God's creation is good.

The SON OF GOD shines brightly. He is perfect, unchanging, divine, and everlasting. He is in the perfect place. He provides light and life to and for His children. He is the center of the Gospel, the Good News. The only life-giving, life-sustaining, and hope-generating center is Jesus Christ.

He, who has the Son, has Life. (1 John 5:12)

We become alive, victorious, bold, wise, righteous, blessed, and holy in Jesus.

We receive all this and more because of Christ and His resurrection.

Christ gives life and gives it abundantly.

He provides all we need, when we need it for daily life. Through Christ we receive power, strength, love, hope, a purpose; and we become a new creation. The old nature is washed away through the blood of Jesus.

As we allow Christ to be the center of our life and the center of our thinking, He becomes the Lord of our life. The Son's light shines brightly through us for others to see and know His love.

He who has the Son has life.

Thanks be to God.

Amen.

POWER IN GOD'S WORD

Thou doest show me the path of life; in thy presence there is fullness of joy, in thy right hand are pleasures for evermore. (Psalm 16:11)

He restores my soul. He leads me in the paths of righteousness for his name's sake. Even though I walk through the valley of the shadow of death, I fear no evil for thou are with me; thy rod and thy staff they comfort me. (Psalm 23:3–4)

And make straight paths for your feet, so that what is lame may not be put out of joint but rather healed. (Hebrews 12:13)

There is unending construction on many highways with many road signs to follow.

There is a Yield sign, a Slow Down sign, a Reduce Speed sign, and arrows to "change lane" signs. There is stopping and waiting in traffic as workers hold Stop and Go signs. As soon as the other workers finish laying down a new topping on the highway or remove the old topping, the traffic begins to move again.

In life, God seems to use the words that we see on the road signs: yield, change speed, change lane, or change direction. His words give support, show concern, and helps us in our life. There is power in His words when we yield to Him and His will for us. Many times He wants us to slow down or stop or change directions because He knows what is best for us. He will not disappoint or fail us. His path leads to a life of love, forgiveness, and eternal life. He will supply all our needs for our journey. We need to trust Him for all things as He guides our steps.

> His word is a lamp to my feet and a light to my path. (Psalm 19:105)

God's word, power, love, and mercy is enough and all we need.
Listen to and obey God.
There is power in God's word.
Thanks be to God.
Amen.

GOD'S POWER
THROUGH WATER

Purge me with hyssop, and I shall be clean; wash me and I shall be whiter than snow. (Psalm 51:7)

And now why do you wait? Rise and be baptized, and wash away you sins, calling on His name. (Acts 22:16)

I baptize you with water for repentance, but He comes after me is mightier than I, whose sandals I am not worthy to carry; He will baptize you with the Holy Spirit and with fire. (Matthew 3:11)

The weather changes, and the rain just pours down in torrents. We drive over the bridge and see the water running off the banks into the river. The water changes from clear to muddy and begins to run even faster. It looks disgusting, uninviting, and mucky. The river is unclean, dirty, soiled, and foul. That water is not good, it is disgusting. However, that mucky water is still useful. It provides water for fields and plants and water for animals.

The muddy river describes our nature at times, unclean and soiled. However, through God's word and the waters of baptism, we become clean and forgiven, pure, and white as snow. We become new creations because of God's life-giving water. We become His light in a world of darkness that is confused, mucky, and lonely.

God's love and blessings abound for each of us.

The power of God in His living baptismal water flows to and for us.

The power of God through water dwells within each of us so we can be a light and a blessing to others.

Thanks be to God.

Amen.

POWER OF GOD'S BLESSING

And I will make of you a great nation, and I will
bless you, and make your name great, so that you
will be a blessing. (Genesis 12:2)

Blessed is the man who walks not in the counsel
of the wicked, nor stands in the way of sinners,
nor sits in the set of scoffers; but his delight is in
the law of the Lord, and on his law he meditates
day and night. He is like a tree planted by streams
of water, that yields it fruit in its season, and its
leaf does not wither. In all that he does, he prospers. (Psalm 1:1–3)

In all things I have shown you that by so toiling
one must help the weak, remembering the words
of the lord Jesus, how he said, "It is more blessed
to give than to receive. (Acts 20:35)

God does great and marvelous things. As our Lord and Savior, He is
always with us during the good times, difficult times, and times of
hard decisions. He redeems and renews us. He gives us spiritual gifts
and blessings. He gives us strength, endurance, and empowers us for
our journey with Him.

We choose how we react to Jesus and His love. We either turn away and reject Him or we look up, believe, accept, and trust Him. It is our choice.

If we reject Jesus and His love, there is loneliness, darkness, and despair.

If we say yes to Jesus, we trust and believe in His words and in His promises to be with us, to love us, to lead and bless us throughout our life. His word is truth and never fails.

Life is still difficult, and struggles still come, but God is always with us, and He will never leave us. That is His promise to us. He supplies us with all we need and with spiritual gifts of love, joy, peace, and so much more. God blesses us, His children, while loving us, taking care of us, and helping us.

We continually pray and seek God for answers, truth, and wisdom. So when we go into the world, we go in the knowledge that God is guiding, directing, and blessing us with His love, words, and promises.

Jesus, our Lord and Savior, blesses us to be a blessing to others.

Be God's blessing to all.

Thanks be to God.

Amen.

MERCY

There is a song called "Lord, Whose Love through Humble Service" written by Albert F. Bayly. It talks about God's amazing mercy that is boundless, undeserved, and unearned. God chooses each one of us to be His children. He loves us so much He sends His Son to die on the cross. The blood of Christ cleanses us from sin, and we become forgiven children of God.

> Have mercy on me, O God, according to thy steadfast love; according to thy abundant mercy blot out my transgressions. Wash me thoroughly from my iniquity, and cleanse me from my sins.
> (Psalm 51:1–2)

It is by God's action, His mercy, and His love that we do not get what we deserve, which is eternal death because of our sinfulness. It is because of God's mercy that He delivers us from the judgment when we seek and ask for forgiveness. We all fall short of the glory of God. We all sin. But through God's abundant mercy and love, He forgives us, washes away our sins, and makes us whole to live with and for Him forever.

> By God's mercy and love,
> He forgives us and renews us.
> He relieves our suffering,
> By His boundless love and mercy.

Thank You, Lord, for Your love and mercy, which washes us and cleanses us from our sin and gives us eternal life with You.

Thanks be to God.

Amen.

GRACE

The song "Amazing Grace" is always meaningful, whether you hear it or sing it for the first time or the hundredth time.

> Amazing grace, how sweet the sound that saved
> a wretch like me. I once was lost but now am
> found, was blind but now I see. (John Newton)

God, our Heavenly Father, loves us, even though each of us is broken and flawed. He loves us so much, He bestows on us His grace, which is undeserved and unearned. He loves us so much, He sent his Son to die on the cross to save us from our sins. Christ pays the price for us, and He forgives by His grace and He brings us into harmony, a good relationship, with Him. A life without God and His grace is broken, lost, and without hope.

As Ephesians 2:8 says, "We are saved by grace, not our doing, it is a gift of God."

Grace is an amazing gift. It is God's love and grace that gives us hope, peace, strength, joy, and eternal life. We can do nothing to earn it, we can't do good works for it, and we do not deserve it. When we accept Jesus Christ as our Savior and Lord, He finds us and transforms us by His love, showing us the grace of God.

> Live in grace,
> Live in God's word,

Live in God's amazing love and acceptance,
Live a life that is Christ-centered,
Live in the amazing love and grace of God.

Thanks be to God.
Amen.

LIGHT OF GOD

> Oh send out thy Light and thy truths; let them
> lead me, let them bring me to thy holy hill and to
> they dwelling. (Psalm 43:3)

God is ready and waiting. His light is always shining brightly. Look, see, and follow.

> Again Jesus spoke to them, "I am the Light of the
> world; he who follows me will not walk in dark-
> ness, but will have the Light of Life." (John 8:12)

The streetlights all over the city come on at dusk and go off at dawn. They provide adequate light for their particular purpose. However, the streetlights shine only in a small area. So only in the area the light shines, you can see, but in other places, you cannot see. Sometimes the bulb burns out and it is not replaced for a long time. There is then more darkness than light.

However, God's light is always shining. God's light is shining all day and night every day. God is listening, caring, watching, and leading us on the right path anytime. He opens and closes the doors, guiding us on the right path for His name's sake anytime we seek and ask.

He is guiding and directing us to a better way of life that is abundant, full, and everlasting. Be aware, sensitive, and listen to the still small voice of the Holy Spirit speaking and showing us the way. Keep watch and pray, follow, trust, and obey Him.

God is the light of the world, the light of life.

Thanks be to God.

Amen.

KINGDOM OF GOD

The kingdom of God is different than what you would expect when you hear the word *kingdom*. The kingdom of God is here and now. It is within each of us, and it is within God's people, those who believe Jesus as their Lord and Savior and those who fellowship with Him.

> Nor will they say, "Lo here it is?" or "There!" For behold, the Kingdom of God is in the midst of you. (Luke 17:21)

Jesus receives a crown of thorns, not a gold crown, as our Savior and Lord. He loves us so much He hears and answers His Father's call to the cross to save us from eternal condemnation. Psalm 145:13 says that God's kingdom is everlasting and His reign endures throughout all generations. He is faithful in all His words and deeds.

God also calls us to the cross. He calls us to take up our cross and follow Him.

He calls us to serve, to aid those in need, to help the homeless, to assist our neighbors, help the sick, help those fleeing war and terror, and help those in trouble.

This is the kingdom of God.

> The Kingdom of God does not mean food and drink, but righteousness, peace and joy in the Holy Spirit. (Romans 14:17)

When we stand with Jesus and belong to His kingdom, we too proclaim and extend His life giving love to others. The self-giving love of Jesus becomes our self-giving love and service to our risen Lord and Savior.

The kingdom of God is here and now. It is God's children working together, sharing the good news of God's love, and working to encourage and build one another up for the community of God.

This is the kingdom of God.

Thanks be to God.

Amen.

NO LUCK

There are many card games that families play. Blackjack, cribbage, solitaire, Uno, and old maid—just to name a few. These games deal with chance. Winning depends on the cards that are dealt to you or the "luck" of the draw. Nothing is consistent; you do not know what to expect or what happens. It is all left up to luck or chance.

With God, there is no luck or chance. God is everlasting, steadfast, and faithful to those who believe in Him. Our ever-present God is consistent, true, and unfailing in His steadfast love and help for His children. He is our all in all, our strength, our power, our guide, our sustainer, and our everlasting Lord and Savior.

> Have you not known? Have you not heard? The Lord is the everlasting God, the creator of the ends of the earth. He does not grow faint or grow weary, his understanding is unsearchable. (Isaiah 40:28)

> I, I am the Lord, and besides me there is no savior. (Isaiah 43:11)

> Jesus Christ is the same yesterday and today and forever. (Hebrews 13:8)

> But thou, 0 Lord, art enthroned for ever; thy name endures to all generations. (Psalm 102:12)

God is the same yesterday, today, and tomorrow. God's promises, oaths, and His covenant is not only for past generations, but also is for us now and even for future generations. God is our all in all, He is our Lord and Savior, our father, our provider, our deliverer, our almighty, our redeemer, our everlasting, the Holy one.

With God, there is no luck or chance. He is who He says He is, and His word is truth. He is everlasting; He is the same yesterday, today, and forever.

Thanks be to God.

Amen.

BOUGHT WITH A PRICE

"Financing Available" is the advertisement on credit union and bank signs. Financing is available for your car, boat, home, or RV. They give you a line of credit and transfer funds from your account—all for a low fee. You just pay a monthly fee (forever), and they finance anything for you, as long as you meet their criteria.

This brings to light once again of the amazing gift from God, His Son. In John 3:16, God sent His Son to die on the cross for our salvation so we would not have to spend our life and eternity suffering for our sins. Jesus's death and resurrection is the price that He pays for us to be His children.

We all sin, except God. God alone is sinless, perfect, righteous, and holy. No person on this earth, on his own, can be perfect, righteous, or holy.

But by God's mercy and grace, we become free from sin, and then He declares us righteous and holy. Jesus dies on the cross once and for all for us and our salvation. He pays the price for our sinfulness.

> We were bought with a price so glorify God in your body. (1 Corinthians 6:20)

God loves us and sends His Son to die on the cross for us; therefore, we try not to let sin reign in our lives or obey the passions of the world. We live as a son or daughter of God. Since He delivers us from evil, our mind is now set on spiritual things, not worldly things. We continually seek God, His forgiveness, and His righteousness. According to 1 Timothy 6:11, we are to "aim at righteousness, godliness, faith, love, steadfastness, gentleness." Live in Christlikeness—His faith, His love, His steadfastness—and be gentle in words and actions. In so doing, we take hold of the God-given life, the amazing life bought with the blood of Jesus, which is life indeed.

Thanks be to God.

Amen.

GOD IS FOR US

Baseball, football, basketball, hockey, and soccer; sports season is all year long these days. Referees and umpires call the games. They call fouls, strikes, unnecessary roughness, personal fouls, and interference. They call who is safe and who is out. They call holding penalties, off sides, false starts, runs, touchdowns, and goals, just to name a few things. According to those watching, there is always going to be good calls, bad calls, and close calls. It depends on which team you want to win.

> Behold, God is my salvation, I will trust, and will not be afraid; for the Lord God is my strength and my song and he has become my salvation. (Isaiah 12:2)

> If God is for us; who is against us? (Romans 8:31)

God calls us and chooses us to be His children; He becomes our father, our Lord and Savior, our redeemer and friend. God is our maker and redeemer. We trust and believe in His steadfast love and mercy and in His unfailing promises to us. He is always on our side and always with us and knows what is best for us, and He does not make bad calls or close calls. God always has our best interest at heart even when we can't always see it, understand it, or agree with it.

God is for us and always with us, protecting us, helping us, guiding us, and directing us as we go through life and as we grow in faith. We can turn to Him for all our needs.

God is more than a referee, He is our father, our Lord and Savior, the Almighty, our refuge, protector, teacher, friend, our dwelling place, judge, comforter, redeemer, rescuer, rock, light, supplier, deliverer, counselor, and Holy Spirit.

He is our Almighty Father, who is always with us and for us and in whom we trust.

Thanks be to God.

Amen.

SHADOWS

A shadow is created with a light and an object. Shadows create darkness, and darkness creates mistrust and fear. Sometimes we live in the shadows, hiding from something or someone. We end up living in fear and not dealing with or facing an issue. The result is sadness, mistrust, or despair.

> God gives light to those who sit in darkness and in the shadow of death, to guide out feet into the way of peace. (Luke 1:19)

> Every good endowment and every perfect gift is from above, coming down from the Father of lights with whom there is no variation or shadow due to change. (James 1:17)

Just one step, one word, one prayer, and out of the shadows we come into the light. God is always ready and waiting for us to call on Him. Allow God's love to enter and surround you and permeate your heart, soul, and mind, bringing comfort, joy, peace, strength, and light into your shadows. Light removes the darkness.

God doesn't promise that our life will be perfect, but He does promise to be there for us and with us through all circumstances. His love for us and the light He provides for us is constant and unchanging. His guidance and direction is unshakable. His power, strength, and comfort are sure and unfaltering. God provides all of our needs as we go through our life's ups and downs.

Hold on to God and allow Him to be our life and light in a world of darkness and shadows.

Thanks be to God.

Amen.

GOD COMES INTO THE WORLD

God comes into our lives and world from the beginning of time—and still does today.

God comes into our world as its creator, as Baby Jesus, as teacher, friend, healer, Savior, and as the Holy Spirit.

God comes into the world as its creator in Genesis 1:1.

God comes into the world as Baby Jesus born in a manger in Luke 2:11–12.

God comes into the world as teacher, friend, and healer, bringing hope and love to the world in John 3:2.

God comes into our world through the resurrection of His Son, our Savior, in John 3:16. God comes into our world and into each of our lives through the Holy Spirit in 1 Corinthians 3:16.

God loves us so much, He never wants us to be lost or alone. He continues to come to us and into our world and our lives with His love and promises. He wants to take away our burdens, whatever they may be, and give us comfort, strength, and peace.

> Cast your burdens on the Lord, and He will sustain you; he will never permit the righteous to be moved. (Psalm 55:12)

He comes into our world with open arms. He invites us in, into His kingdom and into a relationship with Him.

> Behold, God is my salvation; I will trust, and will
> not be afraid; for the Lord God is my strength
> and my song, and he has become my salvation.
> (Isaiah 12:2)

God is always ready and willing to break into our life to provide us with love, mercy, comfort, and peace.

Lord, come into our lives and our heart to show us the way, the truth, and the life and to provide for all our needs.

Thanks be to God.

Amen.

GIVE ME JESUS

May the Lord make you increase and abound in love to one another and to all, as we do to you, so that he may establish your hearts unblamable in holiness before our God and our Father. (1 Thessalonians 3:12–13)

"Give Me Jesus" is a title to a song we sing in church during worship. As we think about those three words, it certainly carries a powerful message. Jesus is the answer we seek.

Give me Jesus when my life is difficult and hard.
Give me Jesus when sickness comes.
Give me Jesus when I am lost.
Give me Jesus when I am tired.
Give me Jesus when new situations arise.
Give me Jesus when I am fearful.
Give me Jesus when I need strength and self-worth.
Give me Jesus when I am stressed.
Give me Jesus when I am lonely.
Give me Jesus when I sin.
Give me Jesus when death comes.
Jesus gives me love everlasting.
Jesus gives me joy in Him.
Jesus gives me comfort in times of stress.

Jesus gives me rest in His arms.
Jesus gives me light to follow Him.
Jesus gives me peace in times of conflict.
Jesus gives me forgiveness when repentant.
Jesus gives me strength to endure all things.
Jesus gives me life.
Jesus is the answer.
Jesus is Lord and Savior.
He is our hope and our salvation in whom we trust for all things.
Give me Jesus.

    Thanks be to God.
    Amen.

WATER

Jesus answered, "Truly, Truly, I say to you, unless one is born of water and the spirit, he cannot enter the Kingdom of God." (John 3:5)

The woman said to Him, Sir you have nothing to draw with, and the well is deep; where do you get that living water? (John 4:11)

That He might sanctify her, having cleansed her by washing of water with the word. (Ephesians 5:26)

Water is all around us. It is in the clouds, the oceans, lakes, and streams. It is in the ground. It is even in our body and makes up 60 percent of our body. All living things need water to survive, which includes you and me. Even in the desert, there is water, either deep in the ground or it can be collected as per survival techniques or at an oasis.

The water that God gives is life-giving, cleansing, and life-saving.

The waters of baptism wash away our sin through Christ. His word cleanses us, forgives us, and saves us from eternal separation from Christ. His water anoints us with the Holy Spirit. His water satisfies our thirst and gives us an abundant life with Christ.

Our life begins with the life-giving water of Christ. Life-giving water gives us power to proclaim the mighty acts of God, who calls us out of darkness into His marvelous light.

God is holy, merciful, and mighty. God is the river of life, an everlasting wellspring. Ask Him, and you will receive His abundant and ever-flowing water of life.

Thanks be to God.

Amen.

Knocking Down Barriers

In John 4:1–30, we read about a Jew, Jesus, interacting with a Samaritan woman. A man speaking to a woman in public. This all happens at a time and place when cultures and traditions say, "No, this is not permitted."

There were barriers in Jesus's time, and barriers still exist today. These barriers include race, religion, cultures, money, power, idols— all things that pull us away from Jesus.

Jesus comes to break through the minds and hearts of all people to show kindness and love. He breaks down the walls and divisions in our life that tear us away or keep us from Him. He wants all to come and see and know the love and forgiveness of God. Jesus comes for the Jew, Gentile, black, white, young, old, the rich, and the poor. He comes for all and the lost.

> For the Son of Man came to seek and to save the lost. (Luke 19:10)

> For as many of you as were baptized into Christ have put on Christ. There is neither Jew nor Greek, neither slave or free, there is neither male or female; for you are all one in Christ Jesus. (Galatians 3:27–28)

Seek God and His truths; learn to trust, obey, and listen to Him. Put away the barriers because as a child of God, man-made barriers should not exist or get in the way of our serving others. Christ is able to break down all our barriers and touch our hearts and minds. When He enters into our heart, mind, and soul, we can go into the world, spreading His love, kindness, forgiveness, grace, and mercy to everyone with His help.

Christ breaks down our barriers. He comes to us and into our lives so we may see and know the love and forgiveness of God.

Thanks be to God.

Amen.

DUST AND ASH

Abraham answered, "Behold, I have taken upon myself to speak to the Lord, I am but dust and ashes." (Genesis 18:27)

And the dust returns to the earth as it was, and the spirit returns to God who gave it. (Ecclesiastes 12:7)

For God so loved the world that He gave His only Son, that who ever believes in him should not perish but have eternal life. (John 3:16)

Dust and ash fell from Mt. Saint Helens on the day it erupted, May 18, 1980. Ash fell all over, and it got into every nook and cranny. The ash was so thick it became dark, dreary, and ominous for days as it blocked the sun.

Dust or ash can be a symbol of all earthly things. This includes our human nature, our earthly priorities, our possessions, and our position in life. All earthly things have short lives and soon wither away. Nothing in this life lives forever.

However, as children of God, we believe that our sinful self is dust and ash without Christ. We, like the flower, will wither away without Christ. However, Christ comes to save and redeem us through His death and resurrection. When we ask for forgiveness, God, in His boundless love, forgives us. He accepts us and welcomes us with open arms into His family. God encourages us to come as we are to Him, then in His amazing and overflowing love, He forgives us, gives us new hope and a new life. We become new creations in Him, our sins wash away, and He gives each one of us life in all its fullness, in Him. Dust and ash wash away, but God's love and abundant life is everlasting.

Thanks be to God.

Amen.

OUR REFUGE

Tarps cover and protect things outside from the wind, rain, snow, and even from wear and tear.

It would be nice if we could cover ourselves with a tarp and then go into the world. However, we do not live in a cocoon or a tarp-covered environment. Life happens. Good and bad things happen to us all the time.

> He who dwells in the shelter of the Most High,
> who abides in the shadow of the Almighty, will
> say to the Lord, "my refuge and my fortress; my
> God in whom I trust." (Psalm 91:1–2)

When we believe and trust in God, He becomes our refuge, our cover, our shield, and our protector against all things in the world that attack and assail us. He promises to take care of us, walk with us on our journey, and to abide with us. Good and bad things still happen to us, but God is with us, helps us, and supplies us with all our needs. God wraps His arms around us, to shield and protect us, as we go through life's ups and downs. He never leaves us. He gives us unconditional love, refuge, and protection at all times.

We pray for God's refuge and protection; and He goes before us, behind us, and beside us as we travel through this life.

Call upon God at any time for protection and refuge.

Thanks be to God.

Amen.

ADVERTISEMENT CAMPAIGNS

Businesses and companies advertise their company and products everywhere. They advertise on billboards, commercials, smartphones, and even on computers.

They try to manipulate and win businesses through advertisement campaigns.

God does not promote Himself or make His presence known through advertisement campaigns. God does not manipulate us. God does not need bells and whistles or advertisements to show His love for each of us.

> For what can be known about God is plain
> to them, because God has shown it to them.
> (Romans 1:19)

God shows and reveals His love and Himself to each of us through Jesus. He speaks to us directly in the still small voice of the Holy Spirit within us. He also makes Himself known to us through others in the community of believers. He shows Himself and His love for us through His word in the scripture. It is up to us to decide whether or not to see, hear, and listen to Him.

God opens our heart and mind to show and reveal to us His love, forgiveness, and hope through Jesus Christ, our Savior and

Lord. There is no campaign necessary. Jesus Christ is the way, the truth, and the life.

Seek, and you will find; ask, and He will answer you.

Thanks be to God.

Amen.

MEND AND RESTORE

Mom mends clothes, hems pants and shirts, and maybe darns socks. Dad glues plastic parts back together or nails furniture back together. This does not happen much anymore because we have become a throwaway society. We throw away broken toys, phones, appliances, furniture, torn clothes, or holey socks. We even hear of "throwaway" and "broken" children and people.

God does not throw us away when we break, get holes, carry too much baggage, or sin. God knows life is hard and we mess up. He knows we make mistakes. He knows we sin, but He still loves us and takes care of us. When we come to Him looking for love, healing, and forgiveness, with a sorrowful, humble, and contrite heart, He is there to love, mend, forgive, restore, and renew us.

> It is the spirit of adoption spoken to the heart.
> Those to whom God is the God of salvation, he
> delivers us and renews us. (Galatians 5:1)

To the believer, God, in His abundant love, mends our heart, heals all our diseases, and forgives all our sins. He renews our life and creates a new and right spirit within us. He renews us day to day. He renews our thoughts and attitudes. He gives us a new self, in the likeness of Jesus, and washes away our old self.

Lord, thank You for Your immeasurable love for us, Your children. Thank You for taking care of us, helping us, protecting us, and guarding all our comings and goings. Thank You for mending and restoring our heart and attitude and for creating a right spirit within us. Help us bless others with Your love.

Thanks be to God.

Amen.

GOD REVEALS HIMSELF

God reveals some of Himself to us. In the Bible, we see glimpses of His nature and character. In the Old Testament, He reveals himself in the creation and in His interactions with the Israelites, when He speaks to Moses and Aaron. He reveals Himself in the New Testament through Jesus and the Holy Spirit and through the feeding of the five thousand with two loaves and fish.

God reveals Himself as an all-knowing, all-powerful, and all-present God.

God reveals himself as all-knowing in 1 John 3:20, which says, "Whenever our hearts condemn us, for God is greater than our hearts, and he knows everything."

God reveals Himself as all-powerful in Ephesians 1:19, "And what is the immeasurable greatness of his power in us who believe, according to the working of his great might."

God reveals himself as present everywhere in the book of Proverbs and Psalms.

> The eyes of the Lord are in every place, keeping watch on the evil and the good. (Proverbs 15:3)

> Whither shall I go from the Spirit? Or whither shall I flee from the presence? If I ascent to heaven, thou art there! If I make my bed in Sheol, thou

art there! If I take the wings of the morning and dwell in the uttermost parts of the sea, even there thy hand shall lead me, and thy right hand shall hold me. (Psalm 139:7–10)

We cannot totally understand or know God. He reveals to us all that we need to know, when we need to know it. God reveals Himself to us as we read and study the words of God, walk with Him, and fellowship with others. The more God reveals to us, the more we grow in faith and in service to Him.

We trust God and in His everlasting love and faithfulness to reveal His ways to us and to light the path to Christ, our Lord, Savior, and friend. He is all-knowing, all-powerful, and all-present. Today, He is still present and reveals Himself to us by speaking to us, through miracles of healing, helping, and guiding us through all circumstances. For with God, nothing is impossible.

Thanks be to God.

Amen.

OPEN ARMS

Body language is a way to communicate without speaking. Someone with open arms appears to be inviting us into their circle. Someone with arms crossed and closed is a signal to shut us out of their circle. Someone with both arms flexed, down and back, with fists clenched is a signals to do us harm.

In the Bible, God's arms are always open and welcoming.

> Thou didst with thy arm redeem thy people, the sons of Jacob and Joseph. (Psalm 77:15)

> Yet it was I who taught Ephraim to walk, I took them up in my arms; but they did not know that I healed them. (Hosea 11:3)

God welcomes us with open arms. He invites us into His circle, into His Kingdom, to trust and believe in Him. In His arms, He provides love for all, rest for the restless, comfort for the sorrowful, consolation for the weary, strength for the weak, healing to the sick, and courage for the weak.

God stretches out His arms to bridge the gap in broken relationships, to mend lives, to provide new dreams, and to heal selfish disobedient willful ways.

> And He took them in His arms and blessed them,
> laying His hands upon them. (Mark 10:16)

God is waiting for you and me with open arms to bestows on us His love, forgiveness, and blessings.
Thanks be to God.
Amen.

MYSTERIES OF GOD

The mystery of Christ, the mystery of the Gospel, or the mystery of faith is not a riddle or puzzle to be solved.

The mysteries in the Bible, many times, just means it is hidden from the nonreligious, secular world. The secular world will not understand the revelations, insights, or the words of God. However, as children of God, He reveals to us Himself, His word, the Gospel, and His promises as we grow in faith and in the love of the Lord.

> The secret things belong to the Lord our God; but the things that are revealed belong to us and to our children forever, that we may do all the words of this law. (Deuteronomy 29:29)

> That their hearts may be encouraged as they are knit together in love, to have all the riches of assured understanding and the knowledge of God's mystery, of Christ, in whom are hid all treasures of wisdom and knowledge. (Colossians 2:2–3)

God gives those who believe and trust in Him the power to understand the mysteries of Christ, the Gospel, and faith in Jesus. When we try to explain God to the secular world in everyday words, we fail. God is greater than that, and we cannot put God in a box.

God is not of this world. He is an eternal God who was, is, and will be forever.

If we could explain God fully, then He would be on the same level as us or vice versa. Therefore, we cannot fully explain God. He reveals His mysteries, His truths, His knowledge and wisdom to His children only in part, when He feels we are ready and willing to hear and obey.

> For my thoughts are not your thoughts, neither are your ways my ways, says the Lord. For as the heavens are higher than the earth, so are my ways higher than your ways, and my thoughts than you thoughts. (Isaiah 55:8–9)

Lord, open the eyes of my heart and continue to reveal Yourself and Your insights to me, as I grow and mature in faith. Penetrate my heart with Your truth and understanding.

May Your love, truth, knowledge, light, and wisdom fill my heart and flow to others so they too may know Your love.

Thanks be to God.

Amen.

I AM

When naming cars, companies try to tell us something about the car. However, that is not always the case.

A Honda Odyssey is not an epic journey, but I guess you could take an epic journey in it. A Honda Pilot is not operating the controls of a flying machine.

A Toyota Highlander is not an ethnic group in Scotland.

A Ford Fusion is not a single entity joined by another through a particular process. Sometimes names are misleading and incomprehensible.

God's name is who and what He is. He is God the Father, God the Almighty, Prince of Peace, and Emmanuel, God with us.

God says, "I Am who I Am and I Am All and in All," (Exodus 3:14 and 1 Corinthians 15:28).

The name I Am belongs to Jesus. He is the one who was and will always be. He is the I Am, the Almighty God. He is the Christ, son of the living God.

I am the door (John 10:9). He is the way to salvation.
I am the way, the truth, and life (John 14:6).
I am the light (John 8:12). He is the way to see the truth.
I am the true vine (John 15:1). He supplies our needs.
I am the bread of life (John 6:51). He satisfies our emptiness.
I am the Good Shepherd (John 10:14). He protects and cares for us.
I am the resurrection and life (John 11:25). He gives life and forgiveness.

I Am is the one who meets all our needs.

He is the one who gives courage to do the work He calls us to do.

He is the one who gives wisdom, strength, patience, hope, peace, comfort, refuge, whenever, wherever, and whatever the needs may be.

I Am is all-sufficient. He creates all things and holds all things together. He is the beginning and the end.

I Am is our Lord and Savior and the giver of all good things to those who love Him.

Thanks be to God.

Amen.

TIMELESS

Everything we do connects to time. Time is a measure of a duration that can be measured by a clock. Time is always moving forward. Once time has passed, it cannot be recovered. Time is very important in today's society. There is a clock almost everywhere, or almost everyone has a watch. If we don't have a watch, we have a cell phone with a clock on it with the time. Time is necessary because of deadlines, assessments, paperwork, meetings, and appointments to meet. There seems to be too little time to get everything done in a single day.

> A thousand years in thy sight are but as yesterday when it is past, or as a watch in the night. (Psalm 90:4)

> But thou, O Lord, art enthroned for ever; thy name endures to all generations. (Psalm 102:12)

> Heaven and earth will pass away, but my word's will not pass away. (Mark 13:31)

> But do not ignore the fact, beloved, that with the Lord one day is a thousands years, and a thousand years as one day. (2 Peter 3:8)

In the Bible, God does not deal in time as we know time, such as minutes, hours, or days. God deals in moments, an indefinite period of time. God uses terms such as the following: "time is at hand," "appointed season," or "fulfill the past." God is not locked into time. However, He is always with us, ready and willing to help us at any moment. And those moments with God happen when we recognize that God impacts our life and our walk with Him.

God is timeless. His love, words, truth, and promises are timeless. God is everlasting, steadfast, and He is for all generations. He does not grow weary nor does He forget His words and promises to His children.

We can take comfort in that God is timeless and He is always with us, now in this moment and always, and for our children and our children's children.

Thanks be to God.

Amen.

ANGELS

Angels?

Have you encountered an angel in your life?

Maybe you encountered an angel but you were unaware?

In Alaska, a stranger comes to the door and asks for warm gear. All that there is, is a sleeping bag, and my dad gives it to him. The man takes it, thanks us, and he is never seen again. (Back in the old days in Alaska, a person always brings back the gift or pays restitution.) We never see the man again. Dad tells us that the man's presence is an angel unaware and that helping those in need is the service God calls us to do.

Martin Luther explains "that an angel from God is a Spiritual Being appointed for service of God." A good angel announces and brings messages from God. They guard us day and night and stay with us in death.

However, an angel that does not trust and obey God, of which Satan is one, is evil, and God throws them out of His kingdom (Revelation 12:9).

> Do not neglect to show hospitality to strangers thereby some have entertained angels unaware. (Hebrews 13:2)
>
> In all their affliction he was afflicted and the angel of his presence saved them. (Isaiah 63:9a)

The Son of Man will send his angels, and they will gather out of his kingdom al causes of sin and all evildoers. (Matthew 13:41)

For He will give His angels charge of you to guard you in all your ways. (Psalm 91:11)

As a child of God, we choose God as our Savior and Lord, and in Him we trust and obey and take refuge. God sends His angels to come to our aid, to help and protect us, guard us in all our ways, and battle Satan and his angels. God and His angels are wiser and stronger than all evil.

In a broader sense, an angel is one sent to deliver a message or word by mouth, not by any other means. So an angel can be any messenger of God in heaven and on earth. Therefore, all who proclaim God's word is an angel of God.

We are God's messengers on earth; therefore, we are angels. We proclaim and share God's word and truths. We show others the love of God by helping those in need and bringing God's light and presence to a world in need.

So we thank God for His heavenly angels guarding all our ways, while we are being God's earthly angels.

Thanks be to God.

Amen.

MY ROCK

Trust in the Lord for ever, for the Lord God is an everlasting rock. (Isaiah 26:4)

Let the words of my mouth and the meditation of my heart be acceptable in thy sight, O Lord, my rock and my redeemer. (Psalm 19:14)

From the end of the earth I call to thee, when my heart is faint. Lead thou me to the rock that is higher than I; for thou art my refuge, a strong tower against the enemy. (Psalm 61:1–2)

Ocean water hits the rock. The rock does not move. The water flows around and over the rock. The rock does not move. The water bounces and tumbles all over the rocks. The rock does not move. The rock is strong and immovable. A solid rock provides an anchor for a building. It keeps it stable and secure. Without the foundation, the building will eventually fall.

Just as rocks serve as foundations for buildings, God is our foundation. He is our foundation for salvation, honesty, justice, and righteousness. God never changes. His words, covenants, and promises serve as a foundation for our life when we seek, find, believe, and trust in Him. God never fails to keep His word, promises, or commitments. No storm threatens our life when our foundation and trust is in the Lord.

If we build our hope and trust on a foundation of money, popularity, or fame, those things soon perish and wash away. We build our hope and trust in Jesus, who is our source of salvation, strength, and refuge. Everything perishes except the love and word of Jesus. He is the chief cornerstone, our rock, to all those who believe and obey. So when the storms come, we stand firm in God's word, love, and faithfulness, which never pass away.

Trust and rely on God's saving grace, faith, and salvation.

The rock is Christ.

Christ is my rock.

Thanks be to God.

Amen.

One God

One God and Father of us all, who is above all and through all and in all. (Ephesians 4:6)

For although there are many so called gods in heaven or on earth as indeed there are many "gods" and many "lords"—yet for us there is one God and Father, from whom are all things and for whom we exist, and one Lord, Jesus Christ, through whom are all things and through whom we exists. (1 Corinthians 8:5–6)

There is a variety of milk and milk substitutes these days. There is cow's milk, goat's milk, rice milk, coconut milk, almond milk, and cashew milk. Cow's milk makes many kinds of milk. There is organic milk, milk from only-grass-fed cows, whole milk, 1 percent, 2 percent fat-free or lactose-free milk.

In the Bible, there is mention of many deities, gods, and lords. Pagans worship many gods, even heathens have beings they call gods. However, they can and do nothing in or for the world.

There is only one God, one true God, who loves, saves, and forgives. The first commandment, Exodus 20:2–3, says, "I am the Lord your God, who brought you out of the land of Egypt, out of the house of bondage. You shall have no other gods before me."

The Lord our God is the only living and true God. He alone is God, and His word is truth. He is the beginning and the end. He is the Lord and Father of us all, He is the Holy one. He is light and love. He is faithful and trustworthy. He sends His Son, Jesus, to be our Savior and Lord, to love us and forgive our sins.

In the Bible, the first commandment convicts us to believe and spread God's word and share it to the next generation. Then they too know that God is the one true God and share that love of God to their children.

We believe and trust in one God, one heart and one faith in whom we hope.

He is the beginning and the end. He is one God and father of us all.

Thanks be to God.

Amen.

GOD LIGHTS THE WAY

Oh send out thy light and thy truth; let them
lead me, let them bring me to thy holy hill and
to thy dwelling! (Psalm 43:3)

Again Jesus spoke to them, saying, "I am the light
of the world; he who follows me will not walk in
darkness, but will have the light of life." (John 8:12)

The blinking light on top of a power line pole, building, water tower,
or cell phone tower is to warn planes and people to stay away and
to not get too close. If you get too close, it becomes a dangerous
situation.

But there is a different sort of light, the light of God. God tells
us that He is the light of the world, and His light shines constantly
and brightly for all of the world to see. His light shines to show us the
right path and way that leads to Him. So when we walk on the path
in which the light of the Lord shines, we walk in His love, forgiveness, mercy, truth, and peace. We may wander off the path, but His
light shines brightly to show us the way back to His love and truth.

God's light is not a flashing light or a warning light to stay away.

God's light shines brightly, calling us all to come follow Him.

God's light shines to show us the way, the truth, and everlasting
life with Him.

Following our own way leads us into darkness and frustration.

Follow God and walk with Him and in His light. His light shines to show us the way out of darkness into everlasting light and life with Him.

God's light shines in us and through us so others may know and follow Him.

Walk in God's light and truth, and live with Him forever.

Thanks be to God.

Amen.

GIVING GOOD THINGS

If you then, who are evil, know how to give good gifts to your children, how much more will your Father, who is in Heaven, give good things to those who ask Him! (Matthew 7:11)

For the Lord is the sun and shield, He bestows favor and honor, no good thing does the Lord withhold for those who walk uprightly. (Psalm 84:11)

Our parents give us good things. Sometimes they give us treats, money, socks, new clothes, love, hugs, great gifts, and sometimes they give us a lot of gifts. Some gifts may be bought with money, and some gifts are not. Still, the gifts we receive are from the heart and meaningful.

Our Heavenly Father also gives us good things. His desire is to bless us and give us good things. Our Father wants the best for us and will always do what is best for us. He gives good things to those who ask and seek Him, according to His love and mercy. We can ask Him for a need or a desire, a job, peace, comfort, strength, healing, or help with finances. We can even ask for a friend. God wants us to know how much He loves us by blessing us and giving us gifts. However, it is up to God to decide when He gives good things and what he gives to us, for He knows what is best for each of us.

God wants to be our Heavenly Father, and He wants us to spend time with Him. He also wants each of us to trust and believe in Him, to seek His wisdom and knowledge, and walk daily with Him. Trust in Him and His word, and experience His good blessings and gifts. Our God is a giving God and gives good gifts beyond anything we can ask, think, or imagine. He gives us His Son, the Holy Spirit, eternal life, grace, peace, joy, comfort, strength, refuge, love, and much more. God gives gifts that are perfect, everlasting, and cannot be bought with money or taken away. Things and money perish, but the gifts of God are forever.

Come to Him, seek Him, ask Him, and trust Him to supply all your needs, to answer you, and to give you good things. The Lord gives and blesses us with good things out of His steadfast and everlasting love and mercy.

Thanks be to God.

Amen.

CAMOUFLAGE

The grass withers, the flowers fad; but the word of our God will stand forever. (Isaiah 40:8)

But the anointing which you received from Him, abides in you, and you have no need that anyone should teach you; as His anointing teaches you about everything, and is true, and is no lie, just as it has taught you, abide in Him. (1 John 2:27)

For the word of God is living and active; sharper that any 2-edged sword, piercing to the division of souls and spirit, of joints and marrow, and discerning the thoughts and intentions of the heart. (Hebrews 4:12)

Today, everyone wears camouflage. They wear it for a variety of reasons. It might be just a fashion statement, or they may just like the colors. However, they may be trying to disguise or conceal themselves or obscure themselves to deceive someone.

Satan often camouflages himself. He tries to look as much like a good guy or the neighbor next door as possible—this way, no one will suspect his true nature, intentions, or purpose. He tries to deceive people in thinking that the temptations or the dangers of their choices is not dangerous and does not carry consequences. He tries to make their choices—such as gambling, speeding, cheating, or lying—appear pleasurable. But in reality, these choices and many others become serious, dangerous, and carry dire consequences.

God does not deceive, lie, cover up, or hide himself or manipulate us. God's word and His promises are true, pure, and honest. He wants the best for us and is always guarding, protecting, revealing, guiding, and directing us to a better path. God blesses us and gives us the spirit of discernment. It is this and the indwelling of the Holy Spirit that helps us know the difference between deception and potentially harmful choices and good choices.

> And it is my prayer that your love may abound more and more, with knowledge and all discernment. (Philippians 1:9)

Hear God's voice, listen to His words, follow Him, and experience the love of God that abounds with all wisdom, knowledge, truth, and discernment.

Thanks be to God.

Amen.

ALWAYS READY

Now to Him, who is able to keep us from falling and to present you without blemish before the presence of His glory with rejoicing. (Jude 1:24)

Have you not known? Have you not heard? The Lord is the everlasting God, the creator, of the ends of the earth. He does not faint, or grow weary, His understanding is unsearchable. (Isaiah 40:28)

The steadfast love of the Lord is from everlasting to everlasting, upon those who keep His covenant and remember to do His commandments. (Psalm 103:17)

The Energizer Bunny never runs out of energy, that is, if you believe the commercial on the television. But you must get the Energizer batteries for the bunny to keep going.

So as long as the go switch is on, the bunny keeps going, but still the batteries will run down and die. When the batteries die, the bunny stops going. It runs out of energy, and it is not ready to go until new batteries are inserted.

However, God is always ready. He never runs out of energy. He never runs out of love, light, blessings, forgiveness, power, peace, or joy. He is the source of all our needs, and His supply is everlasting and boundless. God is and has all power, knowledge, wisdom, and love. He is always ready and willing to love us, to care for us, and to supply all our needs, no matter how big or small. God does not depend on batteries or material things of any kind.

Call on God, trust and obey Him. Pray and ask Him to supply all your needs, and do not count anything too small, too large, or too insignificant for Him. He is able to do far more and above anything we can ask or think. He cares for us, surrounds us, shields us, and protects us. He fights for us, helps solve our problems, and keeps us from falling. He does this and more because of His steadfast and everlasting love for us.

God is always ready. Trust and obey Him. He is ready, willing, and able to help, to assist, to restore, to mend, to shield, and to do whatever we need. He alone is God, our Heavenly Father, who is waiting for us to seek Him and to ask in His name. He is all-power-ful. He is ready. Therefore, ask and receive, according to His steadfast love and mercy.

Thanks be to God.

Amen.

ONE TRUE GOD

It is impossible to fully understand and grasp God. God is all-powerful, all-knowing, and all-present. But even so, when God speaks and says it is so, it is so, it is true. There is power in His words and promises. He is the giver of all good things. He is the giver of spiritual gifts and blessings. He attends to all of us in need, no matter when or where.

He attends to our heart, mind, soul, and body in love and responds to each individual according to His promise. Our God is an awesome God.

Lord, help us remember You are the same God and Father of us all. Thank You for taking care of all of us. Thank You for supplying and equipping our every need and sustaining us on our journey. Help us remember there is power in Your love and words. Thank You for being a God of love, light, and truth. Help us to trust in You, in Your love, power, and might. Help us to keep You as our God and center of our life.

Thanks be to God.

Amen.

SECTION 2

The Boundless Love of God

GOD IS LOVE

God is love. His creation of everything is out of love. He sends His Son to die on the cross to save us, His children, from sin and death. "Even though we were yet sinners Christ died for us" (Romans 5:8). God forgives us, and He gives us eternal life with Him, all out of His love.

God is love.
God is love. That is who He is.
God's love is steadfast, sure, and immovable.
God's love is patient, kind, gentle, enduring, and forgiving.
God's love is never boastful or proud, never haughty or selfish or rude.
God's love is a giving love and does not demand its own way.
God's love is not touchy or irritable or keeps score.
God's love is never glad about injustice.
God's love thinks of others first.
God's love involves faithfulness, commitment, and it willingly flows
    from His unconditional love.
God's love is a divine love that is undeserved and unconditional and
    unfathomable and given freely.

God loves us no matter our weaknesses, our selfishness, our sinfulness, or our frailties.

He loves us even when we stray from Him. We are unworthy, yet He loves us. God loves us, the unlovable and the unlovely, not because we deserve it, but because God is love. He loves us so much

He wants to be in relationship with us. So He provides a way to be in relationship with Him through Jesus. So when we believe and trust in Jesus as our Savior and Lord, we become children of God and then heirs. And nothing can separate us from His love. God's love is irrevocable.

He made each of us and loves us with all our shortcomings and issues. He wants us to believe and trust in Him and be our Savior and Lord. When we seek Him with a forgiving and humble heart, He forgives, comforts, grants us peace, comfort, and rest.

He loves, cares, helps, guards, protects, and blesses us because of His unconditional and boundless love.

God's boundless love is difficult for us to understand. We only understand some of the depth and breadth of His love for us. But His love is so great, He knows how many hairs are on top of our head. He loves us so much, He knows all about us. He knows all the good and all the bad and still loves us. This truly is a God of love and mercy and a blessing to us.

May these meditations, talks, prayers, and insights be a blessing to you.

POWER OF GOD'S LOVE

The sacrifice acceptable to God is a broken spirit;
a broken and contrite heart, O God, thou wilt
not despise. (Psalm 51:17)

This is my commandment, that you love one
another as I loved you. (John 15:12)

On road trips, the big rigs as well as the little cars throw rocks at our
car window as we drive down the road. First there is one, then two,
and then three chips in the window. The last rock hits hard, the window
cracks, but stays intact as we continue to drive.

We too acquire chips, cracks, and rough edges in our life. God
continues to love us with all our flaws. Through the power of God's
love, He renews, polishes, refines, and smoothens our rough edges.

The power of God's love in us softens our hearts to love others
as He loves us.

Thanks be to God.

Amen.

POWER IN GOD'S PROMISES

If I take wings of the morning and dwell in the uttermost parts of the sea, even there thy hand shall lead me, and thy right hand shall hold me. (Psalm 139:9–10)

Fear not, for I am with you, be not dismayed for I am your God; I will strengthen you, I will help you, I will uphold you with my victorious right hand. (Isaiah 41:10)

No, in all things we are more than conquerors through him who loved us. For I am sure that neither death, nor life, nor angels, nor principalities, nor things present, nor things to come, nor powers, nor height, nor depth, nor anything else in all creation, will be able to separate us from the love of God in Christ Jesus our Lord. (Romans 8:37–39)

It is dark outside, and it is pouring down rain. Then all of a sudden, when you least expect it, the sun shines through the dark menacing clouds. The sun shines ever so slightly, just barely peeking through the clouds. Then slowly the sun breaks completely through the clouds. Sunshine prevails with its rays providing light and warmth that surrounds us. The sun is always there but not always seen, but it is still there.

It is the same for us. When tough or difficult times come, and they will come, God is always there steadfast and true. We do not always see, hear, or believe He is walking with us, but He is, because that is His promise to us. He promises to always be with us and provide for us even to the close of the ages.

When we go through trials and struggles and come through with God, we grow in faith and trust in God. We hold fast to His word and promise that nothing can separate us from the love of Christ. So in rough situations and cloudy days, we walk with God and hold on to Him, trusting in His word and promise.

Walk by faith and in the power of God's promises and words.

Thanks be to God.

Amen.

GENEROSITY OF GOD

For God so loved the world that he gave his only Son, that whoever believes in Him should not perish but have eternal life. For God sent His Son into the world, not to condemn the world, but that the world might be saved through Him. (John 3:16–17)

As for the rich in this world, charge them not to be haughty, nor to set their hopes on uncertain riches but on God who richly furnishes us with everything to enjoy. They are to do good, to be rich in good deeds, liberal and generous. (1 Timothy 6:17–18)

He who has a bountiful eye will be blessed, for he shares his bread with the poor. (Proverbs 22:9)

We say we are doing this and that, giving our money and time here or there. Is it true, or do we just say it as a rehearsed statement? Do we do what we say we will do? Do we walk the talk? We know that where we put or spend our money reflects or indicates what is important to us. What is important to you? Do our actions and deeds speak louder than our talk?

God's generosity to His children is unfathomable. God does what He says He is going to do. God walks the talk so to speak. He loves us so much He sends His Son to die on the cross to save us from eternal suffering and death. He also sends the Holy Spirit to dwell in us so He will always be with us. God does this for us out of His boundless love and generosity.

If God loves us that much and is that generous to us, then our response is also one of love and generosity toward others. His love transforms our cold hearts and minds to warm and generous hearts and minds. Then our actions and deeds also speak and reflect God's love and blessings.

The spirit and love of God moves and transforms each of us. He gives us hearts of generosity out of His boundless love.

Share with others our time, our talents, our finances, and all of our gifts unselfishly because of the love and generosity of God.

Thanks be to God.

Amen.

CHRISTMAS

It's almost Christmas. It is a time to celebrate God's gift to us, Jesus Christ.

A very small package, a great gift indeed!

Many things come in small packages. The size of the package is not important. The label is not important because it can be misleading. What is important is what is in the package. It could be a diamond, a gift certificate, a Christmas card that says more than any material gift ever could.

The greatest gift of all comes down from heaven, wrapped in flesh and bones and lives a life of service that transcends labels. He dies on the cross, rises from the grave, and now lives in many small and precious packages.

That small package gift is the Holy Spirit, which we receive in baptism as children of God. God created us in Christ's image, and we become the body of Christ. He blesses us to be a blessing, a gift to others. He fills us with the fullness of God, and He gives us everything we need to carry out His ministry and to live a life of service. He gives us the Holy Spirit, love, faith, discernment, strength, forgiveness, compassion, wisdom, courage, meekness, peace, patience, goodness, kindness, gentleness, self-control, and so much more.

He gives us everything we need to live a life of service to the Lord.

Do we use and share these gifts or give them away, or do we hold on to them?

Do we live, walk, and serve the Lord according to the grace and gifts He give us?

The spirit of the Lord awaken us, refreshes, and renews us. The Spirit shows us how to use the gifts He gives when we pray and when we read and study the scripture. The Spirit helps us show Christ's love to others through our actions and deeds and when we encourage one another and live a life of service.

Let Christ light up our lives.

Let our service and ministry grow and glorify God.

A small package, but a great gift indeed.

Merry Christmas.

Thanks be to God.

Amen.

CHRIST IS THE SAME

In life, many changes, discussions, and decisions become discussed and made. Some decisions seem to be made easily, and others take longer and seem more difficult to resolve. But through all these instances, there is one constant, Jesus. Jesus is always ready and willing to hear and answer our prayers. He continues to open and close doors as He guides and directs us through our circumstances and decisions, throughout our entire life, when we seek Him.

> Jesus Christ is the same yesterday, today, and tomorrow. (Hebrew 13:8)

> For I the Lord do not change: therefore O children of Jacob are not consumed. (Malachi 3:6)

> Forever, O Lord your word is firmly fixed in the heavens. (Psalm 119:89)

Christ is in the midst of our confusion, fear, joy, sadness, and anxiety, helping us through our struggles. He never leaves us alone. His boundless love and faithfulness is constant. His love, word, and promises stand steadfast forever. He continually walks with us and beside us and will even carry us. He gently guides and directs us on a right path through our circumstances.

Christ and His word is everlasting. He does not change. We believe, trust, and hope in Christ, who is the same yesterday, today, and tomorrow. Christ is always and forever.

Thanks be to God.

Amen.

IT'S EASTER, BUT...

It's Sunday, but Monday is coming.
It's Easter, but Monday is coming.
Back to the office and e-mails on Monday.
Back to laundry and dishes,
Back to kids and time-outs,
Back to meetings and commitments,
Back to reality.

Will the joy we feel on Easter Sunday be there on Monday?

Christ is just as risen today as He was on Easter. He is there to meet our daily needs. He is there to give us a deep joy that doesn't fade as flowers do. He is alive and walking with us through good times and bad times, during the highs and lows of our life, no matter what day it is.

Jesus is there for us every day, whether that day is Sunday or Monday. He gives love and peace all day every day. He is walking with us through the valleys, seeing and hearing our every need and cry, and He holds us close. He gives us joy and comfort.

Jesus blesses us with hope and gives us strength for our journey. Let us draw from the Living Water, from the Living Christ, to give strength for the day. He knows us and what we need day by day, hour by hour, and minute by minute.

Walk the path that He calls us to walk and trust in His unfailing love, words, and promises.

Alleluia, Christ is arisen.
He is risen indeed, today and every day.
Thanks be to God.
Amen.

TOUCH

Holding someone's hand feels good. It makes you feel loved, safe, cared for and makes you feel like you can handle anything.

God is holding our hand. He is holding onto us and going through every circumstance, struggle, and situation we do, without ever letting go. He gives us love, care, kindness, wisdom, comfort, strength, and peace by just His touch.

> Even there thy hand shall lead me, and thy right hand shall hold me. (Psalm 139:10)

Trust in God's promises.

Like the woman in the Bible who had been hemorrhaging for twelve years, by faith she knew that by just touching Jesus's garment, she would be healed.

> For she said to herself, "If I only touch His garment, I will be made well." (Matthew 9:12)

Just think, if this healing happens with just a touch, just think what can happen when Jesus is in our life, abiding within us. When we accept God into our life, He is always with us and never lets us go. He helps us through all circumstances, even when we think our way is better. We may even seek a greener pasture because there is certainly more fun and more adventure somewhere else. We let go of

God, but He does not let go of us and continues to help us because that is His promise to us. God's word, love, mercy, and grace is forever and it is never fleeting. He loves us and wants us to always be His children.

Hold on to God. Hold on to His hand and let Him guide and direct us to a path that with just a touch brings love, peace, comfort, and strength to our life.

Thanks be to God.

Amen.

BLESSING

A thief comes only to steal and kill and destroy;
I came that they may have life, and have it abundantly. (John 10:10)

Grace and Peace to you from God our Father and
our Lord and Savior, Jesus Christ. (Philippians 1:2)

This is a blessing from God.

Another blessing from God is His Son Jesus Christ.

God sends His Son, Jesus, to die on the cross to save us so we might have a relationship with Him and live with Him, now and forever.

When we trust and obey God, He blesses us and prospers us with abundant life. The abundant life is here and now. He blesses us with gifts of joy, peace, patient, kindness, goodness, gentleness, faithfulness, eternal life, forgiveness of sins, and the Holy Spirit. He blesses us with solutions to problems, monetary gifts, and in many more ways.

So no matter what happens around us, with us, or to us, we can be happy and at peace because Jesus Christ is with us. All good things come from God.

As God's children, we are blessed to be a blessing for and to others. As God tells Abram in Genesis 12:2, "And I will make of you a great nation, and I will bless you, and make your name great, so that you will be a blessing."

God blesses each of us. God expects us to be His light in this world and to give to others as freely as He gives us His gifts and blessings.

Seek, pursue, and experience God in all His glory in your life.

Live the abundant life in God to be a blessing to others.

Thanks be to God.

Amen.

REFLECTIONS

Reflections are everywhere. You see the reflection of images in windows, mirrors, puddles, and even off TV screens.

What do you see when you look in a mirror? Do you see your image with clarity, or is it somewhat dim? Is the image you see something you want to see or not? Do we see what others see?

> For now we see in a mirror dimly, but then face to face, Now I know in part; then I shall fully understand, even as I have been fully understood. (1 Corinthians 13:12)

A mirror can reflect our image with all our imperfections. The image we see is only a part of who we are. That image can be dim, distorted, or it can be clear.

We do not see many things clearly by ourselves.

As children of God, and by the power of the Holy Spirit within us, we see everything more clearly and understand, in some measure, as God does. We partially understand and see who God is, the light of the Gospel, and what He wants for us through the power of the Holy Spirit.

However, we shall only see clearly and fully understand on the day we see God face-to-face. Until then, we place our trust and hope in God, our Father, as we continue to do His work, showing love to others as He loves us. So then our reflection reveals to others God's love, light, compassion, truth, hope, and forgiveness, which glorify our Father in heaven.

Reflect the light and love of God to all.

Thanks be to God.

Amen.

GOD'S STEADFASTNESS

O give thanks to the Lord, for He is good for His steadfast Love endures forever. (Psalm 136:1)

May the God of steadfastness and encouragement grant you to live in such harmony with one another, in accord with Christ Jesus. (Romans 15:5)

Our society is mobile. People come and go. We move because of a job on a different location. We act on an impulse, and then our vehicle provides the opportunity for easy movement. Parents and or families move from one place to another. Then tragedy strikes, families divide, and family members move away. Siblings move across the state or country for one reason or another.

God is always with us and for us. He is not going anywhere. He is always calling, searching, and waiting for us. He wants us to be with Him and wants us to rely on Him for all things. He is steadfast and will never leave us, no matter what.

All the paths of the Lord are steadfast love and faithfulness, for those who keep his covenants and his testimonies. (Psalm 25:10)

God is stable, unchangeable, and steadfast in His love and faithfulness to His children.

He is dependable in His promises and word. He anchors us, abides with us, and intercedes for us every time we need Him.

God is the solid rock on which we stand, and He helps us stand fast in keeping the faith and in doing what is right and good. He helps us through affliction and helps us hold on to hope in Jesus Christ, our Savior and Lord.

God is steadfast, and His boundless love is everlasting.

Thanks be to God.

Amen.

CLOUDS

We watch the clouds come and go, float or race by in the sky. The dark and ominous clouds produce rain and/or snow. The light and fluffy clouds are the fair-weather clouds. Clouds are important, for without clouds, there is no rain or snow. There is no weather.

> I have said this to you. that in Me you may have peace. In the world you have tribulation; but be of good cheer, I have overcome the world. (John 16:33)

> Any one who goes ahead and does not abide in the doctrine of Christ does not have God; He who abides in the doctrine has both the Father and the Son. (2 John 1:9)

We can't actually see God as we can see clouds, but we can see His love through His word, works, and deeds. Just as a cloud is an important part of weather, God is an important part of our lives. Without God, there is no salvation, redemption, forgiveness, or unconditional love; and we become lost.

Even though clouds block the sun, nothing and no one is able to block or hide God or His love. It is through His love, words, actions, and deeds that He transforms us by the renewing of our heart and mind. God's love and light shines for us all to see and believe. God is our Father, Lord, Savior, and Redeemer. Our salvation and hope is in Him.

Thanks be to God.

Amen.

BROKEN YET LOVED

Trees break and fall to the ground. In their brokenness, they become beginnings for new plant life. Their broken branches become a sanctuary for animals. Broken trees are still useful and necessary for the environment.

God uses broken things for His glory. In Psalm 51, God says He loves a broken and contrite heart. In the Bible, we see many broken, but forgiven, people. Martha worries, the Disciples sleep when Jesus needs them, there is a sinner and prostitute by the name of Rahab, King David is an adulterer and murderer, and Peter denies Christ. Yet God loves them and forgives them, when in all humility and sorrow they confess their sins. They love God, and they live to serve Him, and because of them, many others have come to believe and trust in God. God loves a broken and humble heart.

God loves us. He knows life is messy and we become broken, but when we bring our brokenness to Him, He is able to mend and restore us to new life.

God sees us through His eyes, through His love and forgiveness. He sees our potential and our possibilities. It doesn't matter to Him where we come from, what it is we have done, or who we were in the past. If we come to Jesus—in all humility, brokenness, and sorrow—and confess and repent of our guilt and sin, He will forgive us. We need Jesus, our Savior, to transform our rebellious, broken, and sinful self. We need Jesus to renew a right spirit within us. That is His promise to us.

Jesus loves us, redeems us, forgives us, and restores our spirit. Therefore, we love others as Christ loves us and continues to love us. We spread His word of love and forgiveness, help and give aid to those in need, give assistance to those in distress and to those who need assistance.

God loves us—fallen and broken, yet forgiven. We love others, our neighbors and our enemies, because Christ loves us.

Praise and glory to God.

Thanks be to God.

Amen.

REAL LIFE

And this is the testimony, that God gave us eternal life, and this life is in his Son. He who has the Son has life; he who has not the Son of God has not life. (1 John 5:11–12)

In Him was life, and the life was the light of men. The light shines in the darkness, and the darkness has not overcome it. (John 1:4–5)

Life. Life comes with a mortgage, a spouse, a job, children, coworkers, neighbors, yard work, love, and anything and everything else that comes with life here and now.

We all need the one true real God. God gives us, His children, real love, real answers, real help, real peace, real comfort, real strength, real joy, real forgiveness, real life, real hope, and all that comes with the one true real God, when we believe and trust in Him, who loves us unconditionally.

Life worth living is life with God.

Thanks be to God.

Amen.

LOVE OF GOD

God shows His love for us in that while we were yet sinners, Christ died for us. (Romans 5:8)

For I am sure that neither death, nor life, nor angels, nor principalities, nor things present, nor things to come, nor powers, nor height, nor depth, nor anything else in all creation, will be able to separate us from the love of God in Christ Jesus our Lord. (Romans 8:38–39)

And that Christ may dwell in your hearts through faith; that you, being rooted and grounded in love, may have power to comprehend with all the saints what is the breadth and length and height and depth, and to know the love of Christ which surpasses knowledge, that you may be filled with all the fullness of God. (Ephesians 3:17–19)

God's love moves and changes us. His love changes the hardest of hearts and minds. When we believe and trust in Him and His love, He moves us to act differently in the world. He moves us to be more Christlike in our thoughts, actions, and deeds.

His love turns our despair to hope, our sorrow to joy and praise, and our confusion to clarity. His love turns our loneliness to compassion and purpose, and our turmoil to peace. His love turns our sinfulness to forgiveness.

God's love gives purpose and meaning to our lives. His love wakes our sleeping heart and mind. His love is true, genuine, and holy. His love redeems us, forgives us, renews us, and gives salvation to each of us.

His love helps us overcome all that controls us, weighs us down, and keeps us away from Him or keeps us fearful. His love is abundant and overflows to each of us. God's love gives life that is abundant, free, hopeful, and a blessing.

God's love moves and changes our life and gives it new meaning and purpose.

God's love is for you and for me.

Thanks be to God.

Amen.

OUR IDENTITY

You need proof of your identity for a license, passport, social security number, and for just about anything anymore. People want to verify your name, address, birth date, age, and even your photo. Proof of your identity is necessary to get a job, cash a check, travel on a plane, or to rent an apartment.

However, we receive an identity from God. He does not require us to produce a license or passport before He bestows on us our identity, a child of God. God knows our heart. God loves us so much that He wants everyone to be His child. When we believe and trust in Jesus Christ as our Savior and Lord, and through baptism, we become a child of God.

> I am the good Shepard; I know my own and my own know me. (John 10:14)
>
> O Lord, thou has searched me and know me! (Psalm 139:1)
>
> But to all who receive Him, who believe in His name, He gave the right to be children of God. (John 1:12)

Everyone who believes that Jesus is Christ is a child of God, and everyone who loves the parent, loves the child. (1 John 5:1)

Child of God, an identity that is much more than a name. We become His heir and a member of the kingdom of God.

God loves us. He chooses each of us to be His child. He seals each of us with the Holy Spirit, in baptism. He redeems each of us through the blood and resurrection of Jesus. God forgives each of us and blesses each of us with gifts, and we become new creations in Him.

We receive all this and more when we accept Jesus as our Savior and Lord.

God identifies us as His Child, no proof is required.

God loves each of us, and He promises that "the gifts of God and the call of God are irrevocable" (Romans 11:29).

Thanks be to God.

Amen.

TRINITY

We baptize in the name of the Father, Son, and Holy Spirit—the Trinity.

One God and only one God that exists in three persons—all are equal and eternal.

Trinity is beyond all human comprehension.

Someone once said, "If you try to explain the Trinity, you will lose your mind, but if you deny it, you will lose your soul."

At times we try to figure out God and think He is a certain way. But we cannot put God in box. He is far bigger than we can ever imagine.

> For as the heavens are higher than the earth,
> so are my ways higher than your ways, and my
> thoughts than your thoughts. (Isaiah 55:9)

God blesses us with His honor, His glory, His righteousness, and His love. God sent His Son to die on the cross for our redemption. He sends the Holy Spirit to each of us to be with us always.

The wonder of it all. Let's live in the amazing love and grace of God our Father. Even if we do not understand completely, we believe, trust, and know in part of God's great love for us, His children.

God loves us so much He provides us with the Father, Son, and the Holy Spirit—the Trinity.

Thanks be to God.

Amen.

PEACE

Remember the song "I've Got Peace like a River"? We used to sing it in Sunday school. Think about that title. Think about the description and imagery it brings of a river. A river flows continually. A river flows through all kinds of terrain and in different parts of the earth. A river's source is an unending body of fresh water.

Peace from God is different than worldly peace. Worldly peace depends on circumstances and is uncertain. But God's peace is certain and constant.

> Peace I leave with you; my peace I give to you, not as the world gives do I give you. Let not your hearts be troubled, neither let them be afraid. (John 14:27)

> And the peace of God, which passes all understanding, will keep you hearts and minds in Jesus Christ. (Philippians 4:7)

God's peace is like a river. It is constant and continually flows to us. God's peace is for all who believe and trust in Him. The source of true peace is God, and His peace is unending.

God's gift of peace is always there for you and me and within each of us—when we receive the Holy Spirit, in baptism. God gives us a peace that keeps worry and anxiety and unhealthy thoughts from overtaking us. God alone is the source and giver of peace that results in a calm and still heart and mind in the midst of turmoil and trials. He gives us peace and arms us from on high with strength and endurance to face all that is before us.

Let the unending peace of God dwell and flow from us to all we meet.

The peace of God be with you all.

> Now may the Lord of peace himself give you peace at all times, in all ways. The Lord be with you all. (2 Thessalonians 3:16)

Thanks be to God.
Amen.

A BIBLE

Someone once compared a Bible to a parachute. A parachute is no good unless one opens it and uses it. Just as a Bible is of no use sitting on a table closed, unopened. One can pack and carry it around, but it is of no use. One needs to open the Bible, read its words, accept and believe in Jesus and in His word for it to be of any use. Once you trust and believe in God's word and Jesus as your Savior and Lord, you become inspired and empowered by the word and in the love of Jesus. New words and a new meaning for life begins. It is a beginning of an abundant life with Jesus, who opens the door to His everlasting love, forgiveness, and kingdom.

> Ask, and it will be given to you; seek, and you
> will find; knock, and it will be opened to you.
> For every one who asks receives, and he who seeks
> finds, and to him who knocks it will be opened.
> (Matthew 7:7–8)

God is waiting to share His love, promises, and blessings with us. He is waiting to give us light, knowledge, wisdom, and an abundant life.

The Bible, the word of God, is for you and for me—open it, believe, trust, and obey it for an everlasting abundant life.

Ask in His name, and you will receive according to His steadfast love.

Thanks be to God.

Amen.

DIRTY LAUNDRY

There is dirty laundry in all the bedrooms. It is time to wash the laundry with soap and water to get rid of the dirt and grime. Time to get the laundry clean so it is clean and usable again.

Water is essential to get rid of dirt. But all the water in the world can't get rid of our "dirty laundry," which is our sin. God uses water and His word to wash away our sins. He baptizes us with the water and the word of God. Through Jesus's word, power, and the water, He washes us, forgives us, and declares us clean. He revitalizes us, nourishes us, and we become clean, holy, and pure through the water and blood of Jesus Christ.

> That he may sanctify her, having cleansed her by the washing of water with the word. (Ephesians 5:26)

> He saved us, not because of deeds done by us in righteousness, but in virtue of His own mercy, by washing of regeneration and renewal of the Holy Spirit. (Titus 3:5)

> And now why do you wait? Rise and be baptized, and wash away your sin, calling on His name. (Acts 22:16)

Water and the Word washes us and takes away our sin. God gives us a new nature and a new way to see things in our heart, mind, and soul. The living waters of God cleanses our hearts, thoughts, and minds and helps us to grow into being more Christlike in all we say and do. God's forgiveness changes our life.

> God is the source of living water, to those who drink from it will never die and never thirst. (John 4:14)

The cleansing, life-giving water of God is for each of us. Drink and live in the love and abundant life of God.

Thanks be to God.

Amen.

WHY TRUST IN THE LORD?

In the Bible, Job lost everything. His friends did not comfort him, and nothing and no one is helping him. He is in misery and anguish. He is not sinless or blameless. The Bible says Job gradually turns to God, as He remembers the past wisdom, power, counsel, and understanding and the wondrous works of God. Job confesses his sins; and God accepts, renews, and restores Job. God blesses Job with more than he could imagine with more than he had before.

> When I am afraid I put my trust in thee. (Psalm 56:3)
>
> Trust in the Lord with all your heart, and do not rely on your own insight. (Proverbs 3:5)
>
> Take delight in the Lord, and he will give you the desires of your heart. Commit you way to the Lord; trust in Him, and He will act. He will bring forth your vindication as the light, and you right as the noonday. (Psalm 37:4–6)

The abundant love of God is for us. God and His love is always dependable and trustworthy. God is sovereign; and all He does for us, His children, is because of love. God provides all things for His children. God is faithful now and always. God is honest. He never lies and never fails. God knows us and what is best for us and helps us out of His incomprehensible and boundless wisdom and love. He proves Himself over and over to His children. We can count on His steadfast faithfulness and trustworthiness as we learn from the past and remember God's wisdom, power, understanding, and wondrous works.

God is our all-sufficient help. We come to Him in all confidence and faith, with all our concerns and cares. In God's hands, He works things out for the best for His children. God gives assurance and takes away doubt. He brings confidence in His power, might, and wisdom. He is worthy of our trust.

Trusting God means being patient while waiting for the working hand of God.

Trusting God means being obedient and letting go and letting God work.

Trust in God, He never fails. He gives us His peace, takes away our fear and worry. He is steadfast and faithful to all generations and knows us and yet loves us.

Trust in God.

Thanks be to God.

Amen.

GOD IS ALWAYS WITH US

Do friends help during your struggles, or do they disappear?

Do friends stay and help when you are going through difficulties, or do they drop out of touch?

Do coworkers stand up for you at work, or do they walk away?

God is always with us. He stands with us and is always there for us. Nothing can separate us from God. God uses situations to teach, to help, and to guide us through life. He talks to us and reminds us how much He loves us and that He will always be with us through all situations. He will never turn away or run away from us. God is always ready to love us and help us find a new vision and a new dream that blesses beyond all measure. Nothing can prevent us from receiving the love of God or the life He has in store for us, except ourselves.

> With the Lord on my side I do not fear, What can man do to me? (Psalm 118:6)

> No man shall be able to stand before you all the days of you life, as I was with Moses so I will be with you, I will not fail you or forsake you. (Joshua 1:5)

> I have been crucified with Christ it is no longer I who live, but Christ in me; and the life I

now live in the flesh I live by faith in the Son
of God, who loved me and gave himself for me.
(Galatians 2:20)

God lives in and through us and is on our side.
God's amazing love for us is boundless.
God's word and love does not fail.
God is always with us to protect, guide, forgive, and to love us,
no matter what.
Thanks be to God.
Amen.

GOD REIGNS IN LOVE

Who reigns in your life?

Who is in control of your life?

Who do you go to for help?

Who do you listen to and trust in times of trouble?

God reigns in love and wants to be our God.

God wants us to love Him with our whole heart, mind, and soul.

God wants us to rely on Him for all things and to live with Him forever.

He wants to be our Heavenly Father, and for us to be His children.

> For the love of Christ controls us because we are convinced that one has died for all, therefore all have died and he died for all and those who live might live no longer for themselves, but for Him. (2 Corinthians 5:14–15)

> For the Lord is our judge, the Lord is our ruler, the Lord is our King; He will save us. (Isaiah 33:22)

According to various verses in the Bible, Psalm 46:10, Proverbs 16:9, John 16:33, and 1 Chronicles 29:11–12, God wants to be our God. He is not like an earthly king or person in authority who abuses authority and brings fear to people. God reigns in love. He wants to help us, guide us, and direct our steps to an abundant and everlasting life. God is able to provide us with all we need in every situation. God is able to give love, peace, prosperity, health, courage, and strength to our life. God fights for us and is always with us. He always knows and wants the best for His children. He reigns in love for His children.

Let God into your life and let Him be your God. No other God listens, hears, cares, and answers the prayers of their children.

Let God reign in your life in love.

Let God guide and direct your steps to an abundant life with Him.

> But I trust in thee, O Lord, I say, "Thou art my God." My times are in thy hand; deliver me from the hand of my enemies and persecutors! (Psalm 31:14–15)

Thanks be to God.
Amen.

Amazing Love of God

God loves His children so much He never wants us to be alone, to be afraid, or to be unprotected in our daily life. He did not leave us to fend for ourselves in this world.

God loves so much that He takes care of us in a variety of ways.

First, God gives us His word that never passes away. His word and promises are true and forever and will endure from generation to generation.

> The grass withers, the flower fades, but the word
> of our God will stand for ever. (Isaiah 40:8)

Then God gives us His Son, Jesus, for our salvation through His death and resurrection.

> For God so loved the world that he gave His only
> Son, that whoever believes in Him should not
> perish but have eternal life. (John 3:16)

God also sends His Holy Spirit to abide with us and be with us through all our life.

> Do you not know that you are God's temple and
> that God's spirit dwells in you? (1 Corinthians
> 3:16)

And God gives us His angels to guard us in all our ways.

> For He will give His Angels charge of you to
> guard you in all your ways. (Psalm 91:11)

God provides for His children. He is always with us and His steadfast love for us endures forever (Psalm 136:1). His word and promise He gives His children is trustworthy and always. He will protect those who call upon His name (2 Samuel 22:31). God wants to give us all this and more—more than we can think or imagine (James 1:12).

No one and nothing can separate us from the love of God, except ourselves.

God, in His infinite love and wisdom, sends us Jesus to be our Savior and Lord. He sends us His word found in the Bible. He sends us the Holy Spirit to abide within us and interpret the word for us. And He sends His angels to guard us in all our ways and protect us against all evil.

God's steadfast love is always and forever for us, and it never fails. God provides and protects and gives blessings to those who believe and trust in Him. The love of God is amazing forever and a blessing to and for His children.

Thanks be to God.

Amen.

ABUNDANT LIFE WITH GOD

A thief comes to take things that do not belong to him. A thief is selfish. He only thinks of himself and what he wants and what he can get for himself.

Jesus comes to take away our sin and gives us life. Jesus comes to save us, to give us gifts and blessings. He comes to help us and grant us mercy and grace. He comes in love to give us wisdom and knowledge of the Lord and to give us an abundant life and eternal life.

> The thief comes only to steal and kill and destroy;
> I come that they may have life, and have it abundantly. (John 10:10)

> He will be the stability of your times, abundance
> of salvation, wisdom, and knowledge; the fear of
> the Lord is his treasure. (Isaiah 33:6)

Jesus gives us abundant life the moment we accept Him as Savior and Lord.

The abundant life of God is not about material things but about living a life to the glory of God and His word.

God gives us His wisdom, knowledge, the ability to know right from wrong, and to grow and mature in faith.

God gives us His power to overcome fear and worry and things that hold us back from sharing the love of God to others.

God gives us His love and helps us through all our daily life.

The abundant life of God gives us His joy, love, peace, patience, kindness, goodness, and self-control that changes our attitudes, our heart, our mind, and our choices.

When we live in the abundant life of God, we live in peace and in contentment knowing that no matter the circumstance, God loves us and is with us.

As children of God, we accept and receive God, His love, and all that He wants to give us. Seek God, the giver of all good things, who wants to give us an abundant life and love beyond all comprehension, today and forever.

Thanks be to God.

Amen.

GIFTS OF GOD

A friend gives you a present all wrapped in paper and ribbon. You excitedly receive it, open it, and thank them. And so the present becomes of value to you no matter what it is because of the giver, who gives the present willingly and in love. Some gifts, however, become insignificant, meaningless, or unwanted. These gifts get put away, given away, or thrown out.

> Grace was given to each of us according to the measure of Christ's gift. (Ephesians 4:7)

> All these (gifts) are inspired by one and the same spirit who apportions to each one individually as He wills. (1 Corinthians 12:11)

> I wish that all were as I myself am. But each has his own special gift from God, one of one kind and one of another. (1 Corinthians 7:7)

> The gifts and call of God are irrevocable. (Romans 11:29)

God blesses us and gives us gifts out of His great love for us. He bestows on His children gifts of grace and mercy, the Holy Spirit, forgiveness, eternal life, the fruits of the Spirit (which includes joy, peace, patience, kindness, gentleness, and self-control), wisdom, knowledge, and many more. He bestows on each of His children their own gifts.

The gifts we receive from God become the most valued gifts we ever receive. He gives them willingly and out of love. Therefore, we become good stewards of those gifts through prayer and with God's help. Then we use the gifts given to build up one another, encourage others, and serve a world in need. As 1 Peter 4:10 says, as we receive a gift, we are to use it for one another, as this is what a good steward of God's gifts and grace is all about.

Everything we have is a gift from God, but Satan wants you to believe otherwise and wants you to devalue all those gifts. Our God is a great God who blesses His children with love and gifts beyond our understanding. God blesses us and gives us His greatest gift of all, Jesus, who is our Lord and Savior, the one who was, is, and is to come. The gifts of God are everlasting.

Be good stewards of the gifts given to us by God.

Thanks be to God.

Amen.

GOOD GIFTS FROM GOD

Blessed be the God and Father of our Lord
Jesus Christ, who has blessed us in Christ with
every spiritual blessing in the heavenly places.
(Ephesians 1:3)

The Lord bless and keep you. (Numbers 6:24)

Every good endowment and every perfect gift
is from above, coming down from the Father of
Lights with whom there is no variation or shadow
due to change. (James 1:17)

We live in a world where material things, money, and power are very important to people. But Jesus shows us another way. A way that focuses on Jesus and His way of life. A life where material wealth is not the most important thing in life. It is okay to gain material wealth, but it is not to be the main focus of our life. Jesus's love, light, and truth is the priority, and then everything else falls into place.

When we put Jesus first, trust and believe in Him; and when we seek and obey His words, God takes delight in this and blesses us. God blesses us with everyday things we need, such as a job, good health, family, friends, food, and more. He also blesses us with spiritual gifts, such as peace, patience, kindness, humility, goodness and joy, comfort, and strength and more.

Every good and perfect gift is from God. We continue to strive to be more Christlike in all our actions and deeds with God's help. We count our blessings daily and thank God for all our blessings and good gifts. When we become good stewards of God's gifts, others see our gifts in action and know Jesus and His love.

The Lord bless you with His good gifts.

Thanks be to God.

Amen.

God Is the Answer

My grace is sufficient for you, for my power is made perfect in weakness. I will all the more gladly boast of my weaknesses, that the power of Christ may rest upon me. For the sake of Christ, then, I am content with weaknesses, insults, hardships, persecutions, and calamities; for when I am weak, then I am strong. (2 Corinthians 12:9–10)

Patches appear all over the streets and roads. New black tar fills the cracks, the potholes, and gaps in the pavement in the streets. The tar seals up the gaps and cracks—that way, water and weeds cannot sneak through, only to break down the new pavement on the street.

Holes, cracks, and gaps appear in our lives as well. We struggle with everyday stress, a demanding boss, an empty relationship, cranky children, lack of money, or health issues. But God is there for each of us, to help and to fill the holes or gaps in our life. God is able to fill whatever the weakness or the need. When we feel unworthy, depressed, or inadequate, remember, God is there. God is the answer. He is able to provide us with love, patience, kindness, gentleness, strength, healing, and comfort. Whatever the need, God is the only one that can adequately fulfill those needs. God is the answer.

> But He said to me, "My grace is sufficient for you, for my power is made perfect in weakness." I will all the more gladly boast of my weaknesses, that the power of Christ may rest upon me. For the sake of Christ, than, I am content with weaknesses, insults, hardships, persecutions, and calamities; for when I am weak, than I am strong. (2 Corinthians 12:9–10)

God is our strength, our power, and our supplier of all things on heaven and earth. He covers us with His grace and fills us with His mercy, forgiveness, wholeness, and love. God is the answer.

Thanks be to God.

Amen.

HOME

"At that time I will bring you home, at the time when I gather you together; yea, I will make you renowned and praised among all the peoples of the earth. When I restore your fortunes before you eyes," says the Lord. (Zephaniah 3:20)

Jesus answered him, "If a man loves me, he will keep my word, and my Father will love him, and we will come to him and make our home with him." (John 14:23)

For we know that if the earthly tent we live in is destroyed, we have a building from God, a house not made with hands eternal in the heavens. (2 Corinthians 5:1)

There seems to be many idioms about a home.

> Home is where you hang your hat.
> Home is where your heart is.
> Home is where your family is.
> Home is wherever you make it.

Where is your home? Everyone longs to be home. But home is not necessarily a place or a house. It is hugs, kisses, love, and laughter. It is the smell of cookies and brownies baking. It is laughing, crying, screaming, and singing without judgment. It is kindness, gentleness, and loving behavior among disagreements and arguments.

People long to be home, safe and secure and where love abounds. Our true home is in and with Jesus. Jesus is unconditional love. Jesus is safe and secure. Jesus is the center and anchor of our life. Jesus is our mental, emotional, and spiritual safe place. We long to be home with Jesus, whether here on earth or in heaven. Jesus, our Savior and Lord, brings and gives us love, light, stability, security, and life. Jesus is our home.

Thanks be to God.

Amen.

POOR

As for me, I am poor and needy, but the Lord takes thought of me. Thou art my help and my deliverer; do not tarry O my God! (Psalm 40:17)

Likewise, the spirit helps us in our weakness; for we do not know how to pray as we ought, but the spirit himself intercedes for us with sighs to deep for words. (Romans 8:26)

For the foolishness of God is wiser than men, and the weakness of God is stronger than men. (1 Corinthians 1:25)

We all become poor and needy or lack an adequate supply of one thing or another sometime in our life. We may be poor in health, poor in mind, poor in love, poor in finances, poor in emotions, poor in attitude, or poor in strength. At various times in our life, we become poor or needy.

However, with God, there is no need to be afraid of our needs or our weaknesses. God pours out His love, peace, comfort, understanding, wisdom, mercy, and strength to each of us. He fills our neediness, our weaknesses, and our emptiness. He helps us through all our hardships and circumstances. He does all of this out of His steadfast and abiding love.

With the Lord, we are never poor or in need. He hears and answers our prayers and cries. The Lord is there for us and our very present help, deliverer, and strength in all circumstances.

> For the sake of Christ, than I am content with weaknesses, insults, hardship, persecutions, and calamities; for when I am weak, than I am strong. (2 Corinthians 12:10)

Thanks be to God.
Amen.

Our Very Present Help

God is our refuge and strength, a very present help in trouble. (Psalm 46:1)

Hence we can confidently say, "The Lord is my helper, I will not be afraid; what can man do to me?" (Hebrews 13:6)

And we exhort you, brethren, admonish the idle, encourage the fainthearted, help the weak, be patient with them all. See that none of you repay evil for evil, but always seek to do good to one another and to all. (1 Thessalonians 5:14–15)

In today's world, disasters seem to happen more frequently. Every day there seems to be natural disaster, a terror attack, or a shooting. What do we do? How do we help the situation? Where do we turn for help?

We turn to God. We turn to God, our very present help in time of trouble. We continuously pray for God to surround us with His protection. We pray that God goes before us and behind us guarding us on our path. God is the only one that is able to guide and take care of us in these troubled times. He promises to be with us always, through thick and thin, through good and bad times, through sadness and hardships, and through life and death.

God is our very present help. He is our refuge and our strength. He never comes too late to help; His timing is perfect. He is always present with us. If He made heaven and earth and all creation, then He certainly is able to help us, His children. Just as He helps those in the past and those from generation to generation, He is always there and present for us.

Jesus loves and helps us, and then we need to be there to help others. When we follow Jesus and hear and study His acts of kindness, we need to help when we witness or hear of a need. We help the weak, the poor, and the needy, just as Christ did and does.

When we hear the still small voice of the Holy Spirit, then we go and help as the Spirit instructs and guides us.

God is our present help, and because of His love and help, we in turn help others.

Our love, kindness, gentleness, caringness, and humility that we show others is from God working in and through each of us.

God is our very present help.

Thanks be to God.

Amen.

GOD CARRIES AND SUSTAINS US

Even to your old age, I am He, and to gray hairs I will carry you. (Isaiah 46:4)

I lie down and sleep; I wake again for the Lord sustains me. (Psalm 3:5)

In all their affliction he was afflicted, and the angel of his presence saved them; in His love and in His pity He redeemed them, He lifted them up and carried them all the days of old. (Isaiah 63:9)

The poem "Footprints in the Sand" is about our God who is always with us. He walks beside us during good times, and in bad times, He carries us. God's love is so great, and we are so important to Him, He promises to be with us always. Not only does He never leave us, He saves us, keeps us, upholds us, and sustains us. He guards, protects, guides, and directs our comings and goings. He promises to be with us through sickness, hardships, health, joy, through old age, and even death. He supports, supplies, and sustains us in and through all our life. And when our life on earth is done, He carries us home, to be with Him forever.

God carries and sustains us with His everlasting love.

Thanks be to God.

Amen.

REMEMBER

I will call to mind the deeds of the Lord, yea, I will remember thy wonders of old. (Psalm 77:11)

Can a woman forget her suckling child, that she should have no compassion on the son of her womb? Even these may forget, yet I will not forget you. Behold, I have graven you on the palm of my hands: your walls are continually before me. (Isaiah 49:15–16)

As I remember your tears, I long day and night to see you, that I may be filled with joy. I am reminded of your sincere faith, a faith that dwelt first in your grandmother Lois and your mother Eunice and now, I am sure, dwells in you. (1 Timothy 1:4–5)

People we love include our relatives, family, and friends. And when we lose a loved one, we remember them in our heart and mind. We remember the good times and some of the bad times together. We remember times of caring, loving, listening, sharing, teaching, and sharing Jesus with us.

We remember our past experiences with Jesus when we asked Him into our life and sought His help. We remember that He listens to us, helps us, answers our prayers, rejoices with us, and He carries us through all situations. We remember His reassurance to us of His love, faithfulness, help, and presence with us now and always.

We remember and rejoice in God's wonders and deeds of old. We remember His creation and His deliverance of His people from sin by the power of salvation through Christ. We remember His everlasting love, mercy, grace, blessings, and abiding with His people.

We remember His words and promises to His children. We remember He supplies all their needs, gives them His power and might to overcome all adversities, provides them with His strength to endure, and His peace and comfort in times of trouble. God is enough and continues to be enough, as His promises remain true.

We remember that God never turns away or stops listening or answering His children.

As we grow in faith, we believe and trust in Him and to hold on to His words and promises. We learn from past experiences that He too is always with us as He continues to reassure us of His love. As we remember the past, God always remains faithful, and He continues to be with us, His children, from generation to generation, now and forever.

Thanks be to God.

Amen.

SELFLESSNESS

So if there is any encouragement in Christ, any incentive of love, any participation in the Spirit, any affection and sympathy, complete my joy by being of the same mind, having the same love, being in full accord and of one mind. Do nothing from selfishness or conceit, but in humility count others better than yourselves. Let each of you look not only to his own interests, but also to the interests of others. Have this mind among yourselves, which you have in Christ Jesus. (Philippians 2:1–5)

Do not be deceived; God is not mocked, for whatever a man sows, that he will also reap. For he who sows to his own flesh will from the flesh reap corruption, but he who sows to the Spirit will from the Spirit reap eternal life. (Galatians 6:7–8)

Selfishness is part of our sinful nature and part of our culture. Being self-centered, self-obsessed, and self-focused is part of today's world, with help from social media and selfies. The focus is on promoting our self and our own needs and interests. Selfishness insists on its own way and is sin. Selfishness causes conflict and unrest. It destroys us and our relationships.

Selflessness is a word and an action we seldom hear or see from others or ourselves in this day and age. Selflessness is when someone shows more concern for others and their needs before their own. Selflessness happens only when we believe and trust in God and put Him first in our life. Then and only then do we become truly selfless.

Jesus is our example of selflessness. He gives generously out of His love and selflessness. His genuine selflessness of kindness, gentleness, and loving nature reaches our heart and soul, when we focus on Him and His love. With Jesus, we desire to lead a life of service to others and to help them before ourselves. As our focus is on Jesus, the love of Jesus reaches our heart and mind and soul. Then we in turn become able to love others, our neighbors, and even our enemies and the unlovable. We live for Jesus rather than ourselves.

> I have been crucified with Christ; it is no longer I
> who live, but Christ who lives in me; and the life
> I now live in the flesh I live by faith in the Son
> of God, who loved me and gave himself for me.
> (Galatians 2:20)

Selflessness is the spirit of God working within us because of Jesus, our Savior and Lord, as we share in His love. We spread the love of God through His selflessness to our brothers and sisters, our neighbors, our enemies, and the unlovable. Christian love delights in serving others. All fellow men, women, and children are our concern because of Jesus Christ, who lives within us and loves us unconditionally.

Thanks be to God.

Amen.

GOD'S WORD IS TRUTH

He answered, "It is written, 'man shall not live by bread alone, but by every word that proceeds from the mouth of God.'" (Matthew 4:4)

In the beginning was the word, and the word was with God, and the word was God. (John 1:1)

Jesus said to the Jews who had believed in Him, "If you continue in my word, you are truly my disciples, and you will know the truth, and the truth will make you free." (John 8:31–32)

The day starts out pretty good. Things seem to be going well today. You get to work on time, without any incident. But soon word gets back to you that someone at work makes a negative comment about your work. Your immediate reaction is of anger and frustration without taking the time to determine if the comment is just or not. So, the immediate reaction of anger and frustration begins to reign and rule your behavior, attitude, and language for the day. The day is ruined. There is no more joy or love; it is all gone in an instant because of someone's words.

As a child of God, the negative things other people do and say to us need not ruin our day. Let God, who loves us, determine our truth, our attitude, and our behavior. We walk in the grace, love, and truth of Jesus Christ. We live in His forgiveness and boundless love. He protects, provides, and supplies all our needs even in the midst of turmoil.

We rejoice in His word, promises, and truth.

We need to allow God's love and word to determine our truth, our attitude, and our behavior. We do not need to let the words, attitudes, or negative criticism of others determine our truth or our day.

Our truth is in our one true God.

God speaks the truth out of His abiding and boundless love for us. God is trustworthy, faithful, and His forgiving and redeeming word spreads throughout our heart, mind, and soul. Our heart and mind know the truth because of Jesus and His love. Jesus is the way, the truth, and life.

God gives us our value and worth; let that determine our behavior and attitude, not someone else's truth.

Walk in God's love, word, and in His truth.

Thanks be to God.

Amen.

GOD'S LOVE EMPOWERS US

May you be strengthened with all power according to His glorious might, for all endurance and patience with joy. (Colossians 1:11)

I can do all things in Him who strengthens me. (Philippians 4:13)

In the movie the movie *The Wizard of Oz*, everyone is looking for something that they feel they lack. The Lion is looking for courage, the Tin Man is looking for a heart, the Scarecrow is looking for a brain. They all set out on the yellow brick road to seek help from the Wizard. Along the way, they all use the gifts they have, but think they do not possess. They help each other, so they all make it to the Wizard to seek his help. In the end, the Wizard is only a man behind a curtain, and they realize He can do little to help them.

We all look for something to fulfill us or for someone to help us. We all seek help because we are not meant to go through this life alone. As children of God, our help comes from Him. If He can create the heavens and the earth and help the Israelites escape Pharaoh, He surely can help us. God's everlasting word is strength and power.

As we seek and call on Him, He answers. God is our help and strength when we ask in His name. When we seek Him, He is able to take away our self-limiting and self-doubting thoughts and actions. God creates a new and right spirit within us.

God abides in us and empowers us to be Spirit-led in all our actions, deeds, and services. He empowers us to live with courage, heart, strength, and love—to be a blessing to others.

Rely and trust in God's love, in His steadfastness, in His strength, and in His word and promises to help us through all our life. Our help comes from the Lord, and we lack in nothing. He is enough. His love and strength empowers us for all things.

Thanks be to God.

Amen.

Our Loving God

God is love. God reigns in love, mercy, and generosity. The love of God is amazing, and because of that love, He gives us our identity, a child of God. He is always with us, always there to help us, and to carry and sustain us in our struggles. Truly, He is a God of love. His steadfast love endures forever.

Lord, thank You for Your unconditional and everlasting love, which is always there for us. Help the world to see and know Your love and that it is for all people. Even though Your love is undeserved and unworthy, You still love us. We know that if we seek and ask in Your name, we will receive. Help us receive and accept Your love with all humility. Help us to learn, grow, share Your love and forgiveness. Thank You for loving and for blessing us. Help us to love others as You love us and to be a blessing to all we meet.

Thanks be to God.

Amen.

SECTION 3

God Speaks to His Children

GOD SPEAKS TO OUR HEART, OUR SOUL, OUR MIND

God speaks to His children in love out of His love. God loves us so much He wants to be in relationship with us. He wants to talk and share with us, and He wants us to talk and share with Him. God speaks to our heart, to our soul, and to our mind.

God speaks to us in the written word, when we read and study the Bible. He speaks to us in the still small voice of the Holy Spirit, within us. He speaks to us through prayer. He speaks to us through others, through strangers, through our family, through fellow Christians, through nature, and through experiences. He wants us to hear and know that He is our Heavenly Father, a God of love, our rock, supplier of every need, powerful, patient, kind, gentle, trustworthy, and steadfast.

When God speaks to us, sometimes it takes a while to hear because we don't always know that He is talking to us. But, other times we do not hear Him because we are not listening. At other times, we hear and listen to Him, but do nothing. Still at other times, we do hear, listen, and obey Him. The more we focus on God, the easier it is to recognize His voice, to trust and obey Him when He speaks.

God speaks to us at any time and in any place through the Holy Spirit, within us. His voice and presence is real, just as His love for us is real. Listening and hearing His voice may be difficult, but the more we focus on God and His word, we recognize His voice and His truths. He speaks to us out of His everlasting steadfast love, and He will never deceive us or lead us astray. He is trustworthy. He speaks to us in love to inform, correct, transform, to give words of wisdom and knowledge, and to help us.

God speaks to us about His power and might to love, guard, protect, care, and help us.

But as a people of this world, our understanding of the depth and breadth of God's love is somewhat limited. He loves us so much and knows us so well, He knows how many hairs are on top of our head. We are so important to Him, and He loves us so much He gives us His Son, His word, and His promises, which leads to a life of forgiveness, love, and eternal life with Him. He also gives us the Holy Spirit so we will never be alone, lost, or without Him. God speaks the truth, which gives love and hope to our heart, soul, and mind and to a world in need.

God speaks to us and helps us with our life and with life decisions. God tells us to take everything to Him in prayer. We ask and pray for His wisdom and discernment and help during our struggles and issues. We continue to pray and work through our situations, allowing God to work in and through us and to show us the way. We listen and obey when He speaks to us even when we do not understand because Jesus's knowledge and understanding is far beyond ours. When He speaks, trust Him, for He always has our best interest at heart.

May these meditations, talks, prayers, and insights be a blessing to you.

BUSY

And He said to them, "Come away by yourselves to a lonely place and rest awhile." For many were coming and going, and they had no leisure even to eat. (Mark 6:31)

Do not conform to this world, but be transformed by the renewal of you mind, that you may prove what is the will of God, what is good and acceptable, and perfect. (Romans 12:2)

Speaking for myself—I am always busy.

Busy with work, busy with play, busy with kids and grandkids, busy taking care of business, busy being busy.

I seem to get so busy I don't spend much time with God. I don't spend quiet time listening to Him or time in prayer with Him.

Prayer becomes something I put somewhere in my day or week when I need God. Many times it becomes the last thing on my to-do list.

We need to plan time to talk to God and make it a habit because Satan's biggest ploy is to keep us so busy we don't have time left to spend with God.

So the first thing on the daily list should be prayer. And when we pray, we talk to God in faith and in trust, holding on to His promises. Satan has no power over us when we pray and call upon God to help and guide us. Therefore, we can move forward in faith, trusting God to provide what we need and to give us guidance and direction.

As children of God, we need to pray constantly. Spending time in prayer with God is time well spent. We talk, share, and grow in faith and in wisdom and knowledge of the Lord as we build a relationship with Him. Our day is better because we know and trust God is with us.

Starting each day with prayer, a conversation with God, empowers and strengthens us to live our lives for, in, and with Christ.

Thanks be to God.

Amen.

DISCIPLES

A new commandment I give to you, that you
love one another even as I have love you, that you
also love one another. By this all men will know
that you are my disciples, if you have love for one
another. (John 13:34–35)

And what you have heard from me before many
witness entrust to faithful men who will be able
to teach others also. (Timothy 2:2)

We become God's children through baptism and believing and trusting in Him as our Savior and Lord. We are all God's children thirsting for the Living God. We desire to walk a life that reflects Christ. Christ chooses each of us, cleanses us, makes us a new creation, and gives each of us His light and love. He adopts us as His children and then heirs to His kingdom.

God calls His children to be His disciples to a world that has fallen into darkness. As His disciples, He calls us to be His messengers to the world, to share God's love to all people. As His disciples, He fills our hearts with love, joy, peace, forgiveness, and light. He supplies all our needs for all the tasks and issues that lie before us. God stirs up in us a desire to listen to the Spirit and gives us a willingness to accomplish all that He has set before us, as His disciple, with an open and loving heart.

The ministry of Christ is here and now and the mission of Christ is before us.

God is walking with us, guiding and directing and lighting our path.

As disciples of God, allow the Holy Spirit to awaken us in a new and fresh way to do the work He calls us to do in this place to His honor and glory.

Thanks be to God.

Amen.

Run the Race

Am I living in the world without being of the world? Am I running the race God calls me to run? Am I enduring for the Gospel?

We live in a culture of I want—what I want, when I want it, I get it! We push a button, and we get instant e-mail. We get instant information with texting. And then, if we don't get what we want, or if it is not to our liking, or if we have to work for something, we get frustrated, angry, and we give up. I am guilty on all counts. Am I really in the race?

> Since we are surrounded by so great a cloud of witnesses, let us lay aside every weight, and sin which clings closely, and let us run with perseverance the race that is set before us, looking to Jesus the pioneer and perfecter of our faith, who for the joy that was set before him enduring the cross, despising the shame, and is seated at the right hand of the throne of God. (Hebrews 12:1–2)

Jesus calls and reminds us, as His children, to be different from the world. He calls us to live in the world without being about the things of the world.

God calls us to run the race. He does not call us to sit on the sidelines, give up, or quit halfway through the race. We endure, persist, and persevere through all our hardships and joys of life and do not give up. God is with us, helping us and supplying all that we need for our race. Whatever that race may be—a job, a relationship, schoolwork, showing kindness and love to others, ministering, praying, or worshipping. We run the race, to which God calls us, to the glory of God. We trust in God and in His promises for His steadfastness, His strength, and comfort to succeed. He supplies everything we need so that we can run the race. It is not that we finish first, but that we run together with God and reach the finish of the race together.

God calls us to run the race, trusting in Him for strength, endurance, courage, and hope. We run the race to which He calls us to show others God's love and light.

Thanks be to God.

Amen.

PATIENCE

No one seems to have much patience anymore. We seem to be a society of "we want what we want, and we want it now." Our impatience leads to annoyance, frustration, fear, distrust, and anger. We show these emotions many times when we wait in a line at a store or in a traffic jam, with our children, or with our computer, or with our coworkers.

We need to look to God, who is our example of perfect patience. In the Bible, God is patient with the Israelites during the Exodus. He is patient with Jonah when he does not want to obey Him. God is patient with us when we sin and turn away from Him. He seeks us and waits patiently for us to call upon Him for mercy and forgiveness. God waits patiently because He wants to save us and bless us with His abundant love.

> But I received mercy for this reason, that in me, as the foremost, Jesus Christ might display his perfect patience for an example to those who were to believe in him for eternal life. (1 Timothy 1:16)

> Lead a life worthy of the calling to which you have been called, with all lowliness, meekness, with patience, forbearing one another in love. (Ephesians 4:1–2)

And we exhort you, brethren, admonish the idol, encourage the fainthearted, help the weak, be patient with them all. (1 Thessalonians 5:14)

We receive patience, a gift from God, when we accept and receive Jesus as our Savior and Lord. We are no longer slaves to impatience, anger, annoyances, frustration, worry, or fear. We respond to trials and situations with patience and love with God's help, power, and might. But being patient or acting with patience is not easy. It means we must wait for things to change and trust God to give us and help us be patient. We must trust and rely in God's wisdom, in His timing, and in His promises that all things work together for good for those who love the Lord.

God calls us to lead a life with patience. The patience we receive from God transforms our heart, mind, and our lives and the lives around us.

When God blesses us and gives us the gift of patience, His love and patience reigns in our lives so that others may see our actions and deeds and know the love of God.

The deeds you do may be the only sermon some people hear today. (Saint Francis of Assisi)

Thanks be to God.
Amen.

POWER OF THE HOLY SPIRIT

And Peter said to them. "Repent and be baptized every one of you in the name of Jesus Christ for forgiveness of sins; and you shall receive the gift of the Holy Spirit." (Acts 2:38)

Likewise the Spirit helps us in weakness; for we do not know how to pray as we ought, but the spirit himself intercedes for us with sighs too deep for words. (Romans 8:26)

That according to the riches of His glory He may grant you to be strengthen with the might through His spirit in the inner man. (Ephesians 3:16)

The snow falls white, pure, and fluffy and descends on us. It touches our skin, melts, and runs off.

The Holy Spirit falls fresh and new on each of us through the words and waters of baptism in Christ Jesus. The water runs off, but by the power of the word and the water of God, the Holy Spirit descends on us and fills our heart, mind, and soul.

God loves us and does not want His children to be without Him or without the spirit of light, truth, guidance, help, and comfort. So He sends the Holy Spirit to dwell within us and provide us with the love and power from on high.

It is by the power of the Holy Spirit that He speaks to us, works with and through us. The Holy Spirit speaks to us and leads us to God's truths. He equips and empowers us to be His witnesses. He guides and directs our path and gives our life meaning and purpose. The Holy Spirit even intercedes for us when we can't pray or seek God.

The Lord speaks, equips, provides, guides, teaches, and comforts us through the power of the Holy Spirit within us, given to us as a gift from God.

Listen and respond to the voice of the Holy Spirit, which comes from God. The power of the Holy Spirit fills, renews, and works through us to love, serve, and help those in need.

Thanks be to God.

Amen.

GOD'S POWER TO CHANGE US

> And I will give them one heart, and put a new
> spirit within them; I will take the stony heart out
> of their flesh and give them a heart of flesh that
> they may walk in my statues and keep my ordi-
> nances and obey them; and they shall be my peo-
> ple, and I will be their God. (Ezekiel 11:19–20)

> Therefore, if any one is in Christ, he is a new cre-
> ation; the old has passed away, behold, the new
> has come. (2 Corinthian 5:17)

There is beauty all around us, especially in nature. We see it in the
plants, grasses, trees, rivers, lakes, rocks, weeds, the rain, the wind,
and even in the lightning. To survive in nature, plants and trees have
to change and adapt to the conditions. When droughts come, the
stems and flowers die, but the roots still live. But, we don't see that
the plant is still viable. Trees decrease their foliage, their growth is
stunted, and branches die back.

The storms, the wind, and rain come, and things change.
Lightning comes, and things change.

Then rain comes, and *water* brings new life.

Christ brings us new life through the living waters of baptism.
God changes us, and we become new creations. As new creations, we
look to God for all things rather than looking to the world or our-

selves. In Christ, we live under the freedom of the grace and mercy of God. Our freedom in Christ has set us free from guilt and the grave and from our old nature. He lives in us, and we become beacons of God's light and love. God loves us and wants us to live in Him. He wants us to light the way for others to see and to know of His steadfast love, mercy, grace, and forgiveness, which is boundless and forever.

God changes us and gives us a new heart, mind, and soul. Through His love and power, we have a new life in and through Him.

Thanks be to God.

Amen.

POWER IN GOD'S TRUTHS

Teach me thy way, O Lord, that I may walk
in thy truth: unite my heart to fear thy name.
(Psalm 86:11)

Jesus said to them, "I am the way, the truth, and
the life; no one comes to the Father, but by me."
(John 14:6)

In the distance, a tiny little tree sprouts in the midst of a few big trees
and among a massive number of rocks. It is unbelievable that a tiny
tree can grow and survive in such desolate and harsh conditions.

As children of God, Jesus is with each of us, no matter our size,
the situation, the conditions, and no matter the struggle. He is with
us, and He is always ready to help us in all circumstances, struggles,
and no matter the need.

Then when things appear seemingly desolate, without the pos-
sibility of a solution, we seek Jesus. He is ready and willing to step in
to help. His words and promises become our strength, our courage,
our way, our truth, and our life. All things are possible with God.

God holds on to us and brings us through all situations. He
supplies us with strength and endurance to run the race. He supplies
us with His love and gives us courage to face all circumstances. His
word, promise, and truth is powerful and everlasting. Believe, trust,
and obey in His love and word. Then when difficult times come, He

wraps His arms around us for love and support and help. Hold on tight to God's truths, words, and promises.

Jesus is the way, the truth, and life.

Thanks be to God.

Amen.

BEING IMITATORS

Playing video games or board games with the older grandchildren is always a challenge. The competitive side kicks in, and I do not like to lose. So after losing many times, my attitude and behavior disintegrate. Everyone is watching and listening to everything I do and say. My behavior is certainly not about being together and having fun, but it is about winning. I realize I need to apologize for my attitude because it was not good behavior, and it was affecting everyone else's attitude.

Another morning, I was up with my grandson. He was watching TV, and I was writing down some thoughts. He asked me what I was doing, so I told him what I was doing and kept on writing. The next thing I know, he comes back from the other room with paper and pencil and announces he is going to write as well. The TV goes off, and he begins to write down his sight words for school homework. So together we exchange the words, how to spell them, and how sound them out.

Adults and children watch and imitate our actions, our attitude, as well as our words.

We demonstrate Christlike behavior, or we give in to our selfish desires. Selfishness hurts ourselves and others. Selfishness is sin. When we ask for forgiveness from God, with His help, we move forward to the selflessness that Christ demonstrates. We encourage others and lift them up with kind and gentle words; we help others, give of ourselves, and serve others to bring light and love of Christ to all.

> Be imitators of me (God), as I am of Christ. (1 Corinthians 11:1)

> Beloved, do not imitate evil but imitate good. He who does good is of God; he who does evil has not seen God. (3 John 11)

Lord, forgive our selfishness and help us to be more Christlike. Each day help us to be encouraging and uplifting to others, through our actions, words, and deeds.

Thanks be to God.

Amen.

THE TONGUE

The tongue is an instrument that is used for good or for evil.
It speaks of love and truths of the mind and heart.

> Therefore, putting away falsehood let everyone
> speak the truth with his neighbor, for we are
> members one of another. (Ephesians 4:25)

Or it speaks with vile, curt, and sarcasm. It is an instrument that
speaks untruths and loveless things about and toward others.

> So the tongue is a little member and boasts of
> great things. How great is a forest set ablaze by a
> small fire. (James 3:5)

God speaks with wisdom, love, peace, and compassion. He
speaks, and the wind and waves obey Him. God speaks with authority, and even Satan listens and obeys.

> Let me hear what God the Lord will speak, for
> he will speak peace to his people, to the saints,
> to those who turn to him in their hearts. (Psalm
> 85:8)

We too need to speak God's truths, love, and sing His praises. We need to guard our tongue from gossip, evil, sarcasm, and lies.

> Speak evil of no one, to avoid quarreling, to be gentle, and to show perfect courtesy toward all. (Titus 3:2)

> Let every tongue confess that Jesus Christ is Lord, to the glory of God the Father. (Philippians 2:11)

When we speak, speak each day of God's love and his truth. Speak and proclaim His love, peace, mercy, and grace to all we meet—to the honor and glory of God.

Thanks be to God.

Amen.

EARS TO HEAR

God creates our minds and ears to hear.

We hear and listen to God's word.

We hear and listen to others.

We listen to the still small voice of the Holy Spirit within us.

Sometimes we hear what we want to hear and listen to what we want to listen to.

Where do we draw the line?

> He who has ears, let him hear. (Matthew 11:15)

> So faith comes from what is heard, and what is heard comes by the preaching of Christ. (Romans 10:17)

Listen, not only with your ears, but also with your heart and mind. God calls each of us, and He calls us to be different from the world. He wants us to listen to Him and His word and put into practice and share what we hear and learn from Him. He wants us to talk to all those in need of His love and show them by our actions and deeds God's love, grace, mercy, and forgiveness. He wants us to be faithful and walk in His word. He wants us to encourage one another and to build one another up in love.

Let us hear the word of the Lord with an open heart, mind, and soul.

God calls each of us to listen to His word, hear what He has to say, learn of His deeds, and act according to His steadfast love.

Thanks be to God.

Amen.

It Is Never Too Late

It is never too late to learn to cook.

It is never too late to learn a new skill.

It is never too late to start to exercise—even if it is just to get off the couch for a short walk. It is never too late to quit a bad habit like drinking too much soda.

It is never too late to turn to God.

He is always waiting for us. He waits for a nod or a word of "I believe" or "I accept You as my Savior and Lord."

It is never too late to accept God at His word or to accept God's love, mercy, and grace and allow Him to open our closed heart. It is never too late to allow God's love to surround and fill us with His love, strength, comfort, and peace through all the good and bad.

> A new spirit I will give you, and a new spirit I will
> put within you; and I will take out of your flesh
> the heart of stone and give you a heart of flesh.
> (Ezekiel 36:26)

It is never too late to accept Christ as our Savior and Lord. It is never too late to grow and step out in faith, trusting that He is there to help us.

It is never too late to allow God to put a new spirit within us—a spirit of love and understanding, a spirit of truth, a spirit of joy and peace, and a spirit of kindness and gentleness.

It is never too late to let God into our life and world.

It is never too late to let God's love, light, strength, comfort, and peace surround and abound in each of us.

He is ready and waiting.

It is never too late.

Thanks be to God.

Amen.

MAKING DECISIONS

There is a saying that goes something like this: "Who we are is the sum of the choices and decisions we make and live by."

Do we make decisions by what we want?

Do we make decisions according to whether or not it makes us more money?

Do we make decisions by what God wants us to do?

Do we make decisions by the outcomes or by the way it affects others?

God chooses us to be His children. As children of God, we receive God's mercy, grace, and love and forgiveness. We believe and trust in Him as the way, the truth, the life, and the light. We put away our selfish nature with God's help and try not to do anything for power, control, or for selfish reasons. So as new creations in Christ, our decisions and choices reveal God's love for us and that we love God.

> Put on then, as God's chosen ones, holy and beloved, compassion, kindness, lowliness, meekness, and patience, forbearing one another, if one has a complaint against another, forgiving each other; as the Lord has forgiven you, so you must forgive. (Colossians 3:12–14)

> We love, because he first loved us. (1 John 4:19)

Let love be genuine; hate what is evil, hold fast
to what is good; love one another with brotherly
affection; outdo one another in showing honor.
(Romans 12:9–10)

As children of God, we put God and others first, we pursue
peace and kindness, we care for others, and we encourage and build
up one another in love.

God's love is in and through us. We pray that God's love shines
through and from us by our decisions and choices we make, and by
our actions, words, and deeds.

Thanks be to God.

Amen.

FOLLOWERS OF CHRIST

Then Jesus told His disciples, "If any one would come after me, let him deny himself take up his cross and follow Me." (Matthew 16:24)

A new commandment I give you, that you love one another; just as I have loved you, you also are to love one another. (John 13:34)

May the Lord direct your hearts to the love of God and to the steadfastness of Christ. (2 Thessalonians 3:5)

We have a house, food, clothes, electricity, heat, a car, maybe even two cars. We have the necessities to live and then some. We have more than we need or can actually use.

As followers/disciples of Christ, we turn our lives over to Christ. We realize everything we have is from God. Jesus states, "Deny yourself, pick up the cross, and follow me."

As children of God, we should put our mind on things of Christ, not on the things of this world. We don't need another new pair of shoes, a new outfit, or a new car. We have more than we need, so now is time to put the needs of others before ourselves. We give of our time and energy to share God's love with others. We give our blood for a friend or someone so they can live. We visit a friend or neighbor that needs help. We give away our extras.

God calls us to deny ourselves and trust in Him and His promises. This does not mean we have to give up our personal identity. But He does call us to give up our selfish ways, our sinfulness, and our rebellious self and follow Him. When we relinquish our selfishness to Jesus, then we truly begin to know and understand the gifts and blessings of God and His precious gift of forgiveness.

When we take up the cross, we become willing to pay any price for Christ's sake. We become willing to endure rejection, ridicule, persecution, and shame for the Gospel and for Christ, for He is our salvation. He washes away our old selfish nature, and He renews our life. A life of righteousness, forgiveness, and love through Jesus Christ.

As a followers of Jesus, do not be afraid or discouraged, but listen to His word, trust in His power and love, and live with Him in faith and discipleship. Deny yourself, take up the cross, and follow Jesus to truly know abundant life with God.

Thanks be to God.

Amen.

DO NOT FEAR, ONLY BELIEVE

Many forces in this world take our time and energy and leave us empty, fearful, and anxiety ridden. It's difficult to deal with all the issues in our life by ourselves because we dwell on these things, especially the fear and anxiety.

We need to remember God's words to His children.

> Have no anxiety about anything, but in everything by prayer and supplication with thanksgiving let your requests be made known to God. (Philippians 4:6)

> Do not be anxious about your life, what you shall eat or what you shall drink, nor about your body, what you shall put on. Is not life more than food, and body more than clothing? (Matthew 6:25)

> Which of you by being anxious can add one cubit to his span of life? (Matthew 6:27)

Believe and trust in God's love and power to cast out fear and anxiety. Living in fear and anxiety is not living. God loves us and wants us to live in the freedom of His love and promises. He does not want us to live in fear or anxiety. So through prayer and by His power, strength, and might, and Word, we cast out our fear.

> Anxiety in a man's heart weighs him down, but
> a good word makes him glad. (Proverbs 12:25)

God's word is power. God's word brings joy, strength, peace, comfort, and love, which casts out fear. Believe and trust in God's word. Talk to God and listen to his word. God's word and love brings healing to an anxious and fearful heart. Believe in God's word and love. God's word is faithful and for each of us, now and forever.

Thanks be to God.

Amen.

FEAR

We face fears every day. Fear seems to tie us up in knots. Fear takes hold of us and fills us with doubt and attacks our thoughts. Satan uses that fear against us so we can only dwell on that fear. And then our thinking and actions get all messed up and confusing because it is based on fear.

> For the spirit, God gives us, does not make us timid, but gives us power, love and self discipline. (2 Timothy 1:9)

> For I, the Lord you God, hold your right hand; it is I who say to you, Fear not, I will help you. (Isaiah 41:13)

God speaks to us in a spirit of power, strength, and courage that takes away fear that holds us back. It is His spirit dwelling within us that gives us His power, strength, courage, and peace of mind to live as children of God. We face and stand up to danger and fear, with God's help and with His strength and courage. It is because of God's help that we do not give in to those who have an opposite view from God's teaching or to those who ridicule us. We speak God's truth in love, and nothing and no one is able to deter us.

God gives us a spirit of strength, courage, and power. These gifts enable us to share the Gospel of the Lord, to encourage one another, and to face those who want us to fail and run away because of fear.

God is our very present help in times of fear and trouble.

Thanks be to God.

Amen.

FIRE

Fire burns weeds and improve growth of plants and trees.

Fire burns wood in a stove to keep a room warm.

Fire heats and melts metal to refine it.

Fire heats and melts glass to shape and mold it into beautiful art pieces.

Fire heats and cooks meat to eat.

Fire browns marshmallows for s'mores.

Fire can be a good thing.

Fire may improve the value of an item, make a bad situation better, or it can get rid of impurities or things that would detract or devalue something.

> So that the genuineness of your faith, more pre-
> cious than gold which though perishable is tested
> by fire, may rebound to praise and glory and honor
> at the revelation of Jesus Christ. (1 Peter 1:7)

In the Bible, God talks about refining and remolding us. He compares this to melting gold so that the impurities rise and then can be skimmed off, leaving the pure gold. God loves and values each of us so much that He doesn't want anything to destroy the good work He has begun in us. So He renews and refines us as we grow in faith, knowledge, and wisdom.

God reshapes, remolds, and changes our heart, our faith, and our lives to become more like Christ. Then we reflect and show others by our actions and deeds the love of God. God refines and renews us, and we praise and give glory and honor to Jesus Christ our Lord and Savior.

Thanks be to God.

Amen.

READY

Policemen, firemen, doctors, therapists, pilots, and teachers all train and prepare for their jobs and for any situation that might present itself. They prepare to be ready at all times, for all circumstances, and for anything.

In our car, we carry tools, chains, jumper cables, spare tire, and AAA card to be ready for all situations.

Are we ready for Jesus?

We do not know when He is coming again. He will come when we least expect it, like a thief in the night. We need to let go of the things that weigh us down and pull us away from God. We need to let go of worry, anxiety, fear, and anger and believe and trust in Jesus as the way, the truth, life, and the light.

God tells us to be alert, be ready, and be on guard. Pray, read, and learn the Word, be faithful, spread the Gospel, feed the hungry, visit the sick, and provide for the needy as we wait for the Lord.

Prepare and ready our hearts and minds by reading scriptures, trusting and believing in God's word. Live in faith, trust, wisdom, and humility of God.

If we know the hour and time to be ready, then we procrastinate and only attend to that moment. God's love and light would be lost for many. And maybe our relationship with God would be lost as well. Always be ready for the Lord.

> You must be ready, for the Son of Man is coming at an unexpected hour. (Luke 12:40)
>
> Do not be afraid little flock, for it is you fathers good pleasure to give you the Kingdom. (Luke 12; 32)

God speaks to us about His love, forgiveness, healing, salvation, and blessing that is for us here and now. God comes for all. Prepare and always be ready for the Lord, for He wants to give you His kingdom, which includes His love, forgiveness, comfort, peace, and so much more.

Thanks be to God.

Amen.

KINDNESS

Be kind to one another, tenderhearted, forgiving one another as God in Christ forgave you. (Ephesians 4:32)

He who withholds kindness from a friend forsakes the fear of the Almighty. (Job 6:14)

And the Lord's servant must not be quarrelsome, but kindly to everyone. (2 Timothy 2:24)

Kindness is a gift from God. Kindness is a fruit of that spirit we receive when we believe and trust in God as our Savior and Lord. It is our responsibility to learn, grow, and develop the gift of kindness by sharing and showing kindness to our loved ones, our neighbors, our community, and even our enemies.

It only takes a moment to be kind—to allow a car into traffic, to smile as someone walks by you, to share your excess with those who are in need, or to hold a baby while a mom fits on a shirt she is trying to buy.

God is kind and loving to us, and Jesus becomes our example of how to be kind to one another. God values His gifts and wants us to cultivate and multiply kindness in our life just as God shows kindness toward us.

God gives and blesses us with the gifts of the fruit of the Spirit—of which, one is kindness. God calls us to show and bless others with kindness so they too may know the gracious love of God in Jesus Christ our Lord.

The kindness you show someone may be the only kindness they see, know, or remember. Be a blessing by showing kindness to all.

Thanks be to God.

Amen.

GENTLENESS

Most of us do not express gentleness naturally. We tend to be harsh, aggressive, or rough with others in our words and actions.

> A soft answer turns away wrath, but a harsh word
> stirs up anger. (Proverbs 15:1)

As children of God, we act differently because God works within us to transform our heart and mind to be more like Christ. As children of God, we receive the Holy Spirit, a gift from God. And it is by His power we choose to act with gentleness, love, calmness, and kindness. It is our responsibility to nurture and develop gentleness with God's help.

A little girl that picks up a newborn puppy, holds its head, and cradles its body while stroking its head carefully. She is gentle.

A teacher needs to show another teacher once again how to run a program on the computer. At the end of the day, the computer is acting up, and the teacher that is trying to learn the program doesn't understand. No harsh words come out of the mouth of the teacher that is teaching. She chooses calmness, tenderness, and love to once again explain the program. She is gentle and kind with her words and actions.

The spirit of gentleness changes our heart and mind and also changes our actions. When stressful situations arise, God will help us act with gentleness by the power of the Holy Spirit. He helps us act with love, care, calmness, gentleness, and kindness to our loved ones, our neighbors, our community, and even our enemies.

> Take my yoke upon you, and learn from me; for
> I am gentle and lowly in heart, and you will find
> rest for your soul. (Matthew 11:29)

> But the wisdom from above is first pure, peace-
> able, gentle, open to reason, full of mercy and
> good fruits, without uncertainty or insincerity.
> (James 3:17)

God speaks to us and calls each of us to be gentle. The spirit of gentleness is within us. The spirit of gentleness comes through our voice, words, and actions because of the gentleness and love of God.

Thanks be to God.

Amen.

GOODNESS

What is good in your life? Is your day or lunch good?

Is your child or spouse good to you?

Good and goodness in today's world is relative and depends on the context or situation in which it is used as well as the interpretation of what good means.

The Bible says that only God is good.

> And Jesus said to him, "Why do you call me good? No one is good but God alone." (Mark 10:18)

> The Lord is good, a refuge in time of trouble. He cares for those who trust in Him. (Nahum 1:7)

We see God's goodness in His love for us, in His creation, in His mercy and grace, and in His salvation and in His forgiveness. God loves us.

> How abundant is thy goodness. Which thou hast laid up for those who fear thee and wrought for those who take refuge in thee in sight of all men. (Psalm 31:19)

We too receive the gift of goodness, a fruit of the Spirit, when we trust and believe that Jesus is our Savior and Lord.

> Every good endowment and every perfect gift is from above, coming down from the Father of light with whom there is no variation or shadow due to change. (James 1:17)

Since the spirit of goodness is within us, God wants us to grow in goodness and to demonstrate that goodness to all. This happens when we trust and rely on Him and when we let God's spirit of goodness lead our actions and deeds. Our heart becomes open and gentle to everyone with the help of God, not just to those who will repay us with favors. Our attitude and our words are calm, gentle, good, kind, and humble.

God speaks to us about His love and goodness that dwells within us. The spirit of goodness fills our heart and mind so others may see our actions and deeds and know the love and goodness of God.

Thanks be to God.

Amen.

SELF-CONTROL

A man without self-control is like a city broken into and left without walls. (Proverb 25:28)

God did not give us a spirit of timidity but a spirit of power, love, and self-control. (2 Timothy 1:7)

Training us to renounce irreligion and worldly passions, and to live sober, upright, and godly lives in the world. (Titus 2:12)

A three-year-old has very little self-control. They throw a temper tantrum at the drop of a hat, anywhere, and at any time, especially when they don't get what they want.

An athlete demonstrates self-control as they work out daily and eat appropriate food at a certain time.

Self-control is difficult. Each one of us demonstrates self-control in at least one area of our life, but not in other areas. And if we are left to ourselves, we demonstrate very little self-control or discipline in any areas of our life. We tend to give into our earthly desire and give into worldly indulgences, which leads to sin—and ultimately leads to a life without Christ.

When we believe and trust that Jesus is our Savior and Lord, we receive the Holy Spirit along with the gift of self-control. God gives us this gift in love to nurture and grow. God is our source of love, power, strength, and self-control. As we live and walk in God's word, our actions, deeds, and wants become a reflection of God's love and self-control. We reflect the spirit of self-control so others might see and know the love of God.

God speaks to us and calls us to live in His word and to walk in the Spirit with self-control by His power and with His help.

Thanks be to God.

Amen.

JOY

Some people think that a Christian is supposed to be happy all the time.

However, happiness is based on events and whether they go well or not. Happiness is conditional and fleeting.

> For the Kingdom of God does not mean food or drink but righteousness and peace and joy in the Holy Spirit. (Romans 14:17)

Real joy is a gift from God. Joy is a fruit of the Spirit, which we receive through the Spirit when we receive Jesus as our Savior and Lord.

> Thou dost show me the path of life; in thy presence there is fullness of joy, in thy right hand are pleasures for evermore. (Psalm 16:11)

As a child of God, we receive the gift of joy, through the Holy Spirit, when we accept Jesus as our Lord and Savior. True joy, a gift from God, is deep in our heart and soul.

True joy is not dependent on earthly events and whether they go well or not. True joy comes from God through faith. It comes when we believe and trust in Him and in the hope of the resurrection. No matter if we live or we die, we have joy because we are God's children and He takes care of us in life and in death. We rejoice in good times, in sorrow, and in times of trials because God loves us, He is with us, and He helps through all things in our life.

Joy in the Lord enables us to enjoy all that God does for us and gives us.

There is joy in God's unconditional love for His children. There is joy in the blood of Jesus Christ that saves us. There is joy in God's mercy and grace that is unending. There is joy in God's words and promises.

> These things I have spoken to you, that my joy
> may be in you, and that your joy may be full.
> (John 15:11)

Walk in the joy of the Lord so others will see, know, and want the love and joy of the Lord in their heart.

Thanks be to God.

Amen.

NEVER GIVE UP

Never give up on things, be persistent, persevere, keep moving forward.

Never lose heart. Don't give up until a solution is found.

God never gives up on us. God is always with us no matter what the situation. God never starts something He doesn't finish. Therefore, we do not give up on God, because with God, all things are possible. If we do give up, we miss out on things God has for us.

> It is the Lord that goes before you, he will be with you, he will not fail you or forsake you, do no fear or be dismayed. (Deuteronomy 31:8)

> Have I not commanded you? Be strong and of good courage, be not frightened, neither be dismayed; for the Lord you God is with you wherever you go. (Joshua 1:9)

And I am sure that he who began a good work in you will bring it to completion at the day of Jesus Christ (Philippians 1:6).

Never give up on God because His love endures forever.

Never give up on trusting in God's words and promises because God never breaks His promises.

Never give up on God because He renews us, loves us, and is with us through all things. Never give up because God gives us strength to go through our struggles.

Never give up because God opens our heart and mind to trust a loving God for His help and comfort, strength, and endurance to press on and persevere.

> Out of my distress I called on the Lord; the Lord answered me and set me free. (Psalm 118:5)

> The Lord will keep your going out and coming in from this time forth and forevermore. (Psalm 121:8)

The Lord speaks to us; we listen and hear Him say to us, "Never give up, for I am with you and all things are possible."

Thanks be to God.

Amen.

ENCOURAGE ONE ANOTHER

Many real-life situations and TV shows put people down. They lie and cheat to get their own way or to win.

But God calls us to be His children and to live differently. God calls us to build one another up and encourage one another in brotherly love.

> Therefore encourage one another and build one another up, just as you are doing. (1 Thessalonians 5:11)

> And let us consider how to stir up one another to love and good works. (Hebrews 10:24)

> Let no evil talk come out of your mouths, but only such as is good for edifying, as fits the occasion, that it may impart grace to those who hear. (Ephesians 4:29)

As children of God and as a member of the family of Christ, we are to encourage one another in love. We encourage and build one another up with the love of Christ by our actions and words that are gentle and kind. We offer comfort to others with words of comfort with the help of the Holy Spirit. We put others and their feelings first. We listen to others and help them. We gather together with others in love, fellowship, and worship to bind together, to encourage one another, and to grow in faith, love, and hope.

Everyone is important to God and necessary for His ministry.

Without encouragement from one another, we become easily overwhelmed by the world and our failures. We easily feel God is far away and not with us. We become stuck, defeated, and unable to move forward.

With the encouragement from one another in faith and in love, we build one another up and this makes everyone's life easier. God is with us and equips us for this work.

With God's help, love others, help them, and encourage them with patience, kindness, and gentleness.

Thanks be to God.

Amen.

HEART

That Christ may dwell in your hearts through faith. (Ephesians 3:17a)

Whereas the aim of our charge is love that issues from a pure heart and a good conscience and a sincere faith. (1 Timothy 1:5)

Not in the way of eye service, as men pleasers, but as servants of Christ doing the will of God from the heart. (Ephesians 6:6)

The heart is an important organ in our body. It is also one of the main organs of our body. It pumps blood to every part of our body and gives us fresh oxygenated life-giving blood.

Jesus is the center and focus our life. He is our Heavenly Father, creator, redeemer, and friend, our heart. He creates us and gives us life through His love and blood. As His child, Christ dwells in us, and He gives us a new heart where faith and love abound. He restores and renews the love in our cold heart so we can love others.

Through Jesus and with His help, we see things through His eyes. He helps us forgive others, help the poor, love the unlovable, and show kindness to all, just as He does for us. He helps us throw out old baggage we do not need and move forward in His love. Jesus helps us love others. He gives us a new mind, soul, and life that focuses on loving, helping, and serving others. He gives us a heart of love that is like Christ, through faith. God speaks and says to each heart, "Love one another as I have loved you."

Thanks be to God.

Amen.

SHARING

As a parent, you hear your kids yell, "It's mine." "No, it's mine!" Each child knows which one is their toy. They also believe if they are playing with a toy, it is theirs, no matter to whom it belongs.

Sometimes the same happens with the gifts and blessings we receive from God. It is like the old saying "What's mine is mine."

The parent is always instructing and teaching the child to share. God is always teaching and instructing His children to share.

> Is it not to share your bread with the hungry, and bring homeless poor into your house; when you see the naked, to cover him, and not to hide yourself from your own flesh? (Isaiah 58:7)

> For as we share abundantly in Christ's suffering, so through Christ we share abundantly in comfort too. (2 Corinthians 1:5)

> Do not neglect to do good and to share what you have, for such sacrifices are pleasing to God. (Hebrews 18:16)

God too is instructing and teaching His children to share. God shares His love with us by giving His Son for our salvation. He shares His mercy, grace, and forgiveness to all. God shares His truth, wisdom, courage, and strength to all for the upbuilding of the community. As God shares all good things with His children, so we too share with others. God wants us to share what He gives us to those in need. We share because He shares and provides for us. We share His love, the word of God; we share our time, talents, and possessions so that all we meet might see and know Jesus.

We want to share because of our love for Jesus. And in our sharing, we too find new joy and blessings in Christ.

God speaks and calls us to share the love of Jesus.

Thanks be to God.

Amen.

PRAYER

We talk to other people by using a walkie-talkie, a ham radio, a cell phone, landline phone, or through a text message. The other person will or will not respond. The direct approach, one-on-one, is the best way to communicate.

Prayer is calling on and talking to God. It is direct, and it is a one-on-one time with God. God is always available, ready, and willing to listen. He promises to hear.

> And this is the confidence which we have in Him,
> that if we ask anything according to His will He
> hears us. (1 John 5:14)

Prayer is an urge and a command from God.

> And he told them a parable, to the effect that
> they ought always to pray and not to lose heart.
> (Luke 18:1)

Prayer causes us to look at ourselves, at our gifts, at our needs, and at our concerns when we call on Jesus. We talk to Him, to thank Him for helping and being with us. We pray for others, we pray for our needs, and we pray for protection. And we pray to praise and thank Him for all He does for us.

Prayer is part of our relationship with God. It is based on faith in Jesus as our Lord and Savior, His love, and on His word and promises. It is not based on ourselves or our works.

Prayer comes from our heart and from the Holy Spirit within us, which helps us and creates in us the ability and desire to pray. If we pray when we are ready or feel worthy, we would never pray. So the Holy Spirit helps us pray when it is difficult.

> Likewise the spirit helps us in our weakness; for we do not know how to pray as we ought, but the Spirit himself intercedes for us with sighs too deep for words. (Romans 8:26)

There is power in prayer. We learn the power of prayer through our experiences with God, through our faith, and our trust in God's promises and word. Whatever we need, we ask God in prayer, and He promises to answer according to His steadfast love.

As God tells us in James 5:16, "Therefore confess your sins to one another, and pray for one another, that you may be healed. The prayer of a righteous man has great power in its effects."

Prayer is talking directly to God. We do not need an intercessor or a go-between. God hears, listens, and answers a true prayer from the heart. It pleases God when we call on Him and talk to Him.

Pray with confidence in Jesus's name, and our prayer is never in vain.

Thanks be to God.

Amen.

AFFLICTION

Look on my affliction and deliver me, for I do
not forget the law. (Psalm 119:153)

This is my comfort in my affliction that thy
promise gives me life. (Psalm 119:50)

Affliction is something that causes pain or suffering. Our affliction
may be a dead-end job, an illness, a disease, or anxiety issues. Our
affliction may be mental, physical, trials in a relationship, or money
issues. No matter the affliction, we think we are stuck with the affliction forever. This type of thinking defeats us. We become full of self-
pity and even get angry with God. This is exactly what Satan wants
us to do. He wants us to turn away from God and His help.

But God wants us to turn to Him for help. And when we turn
to Him for help, He promises to answer us. He reassures us of His
love and power and to always be with us. Through prayer and reading of the scriptures, God reassures us that He is there for us, He will
help us, and that we can rely on Him for all things.

Then they cried to the Lord in their trouble, and
he delivered them from their distress. (Psalm
107:6)

Blessed is the man who endures trial, for when he has stood the test he will receive the crown of life which God has promised to those who love Him. (James 1:12)

Who comforts us in all our afflictions, so that we may be able to comfort those who are in any affliction, with the comfort with which we ourselves are comforted by God. (2 Corinthians 1:4)

No matter the affliction, God delivers us from them all, in His way and in His time. In the process, we learn to wait, trust, and rely in His almighty power and steadfast love. And in the process, it brings us closer to Him. When we rely on our own wisdom and understanding, the outcome is entirely different.

God reveals His faithfulness, strength, and love for us as we walk together daily. He never fails, and He never leaves us. So as we persevere and endure through our affliction, God comforts and reassures us of His help and love daily. Then God calls us to speak, to comfort, and to reassure others through their affliction of the Lord's steadfast love and mercy.

God is our strength, our comfort, and our deliverer when we cry to Him.

Thanks be to God.

Amen.

OPEN AND CLOSE DOORS

> Ask, and it will be given to you; seek, and you will find; knock, and it will be opened to you. For every one who asks receives, and he who seeks finds, and to him who knocks it will be opened. (Matthew 7:7–8)

> And I will place on his shoulder the key of the house of David; he shall open, and none shall shut; and he shall shut and none shall open. (Isaiah 22:22)

> I know your works, Behold, I have set before you an open door, which no one is able to shut; I know that you have but little power, and yet you have kept my word and have not denied my name. (Revelations 3:8)

We build houses with registers on the floor or in the ceiling to let air flow through the house to heat or to cool it. When a room gets too hot or too cold, there is a decision on whether to open or close a register. This process hopefully gets the air to flow to the right room, but this is not always successful.

God too opens and closes doors in our life. We ask and pray for His help for many situations in our life. When we listen and trust

Him, He shows us the way, He opens or closes doors on our path. We need to be aware and willing to hear the voice of the Holy Spirit and to be sensitive and responsive to Him as He opens and closes doors on our path. God loves us and wants the best for us. He guides and directs our path to a better way, to a better life, or to a way that helps make our dreams come true. God may also lead us on a way that protects us from harm. He is the giver of our life and all good things, as He opens and closes doors and directs us to a new path. This path leads to opportunities that we were not aware of or maybe we thought were impossible. But with God, nothing is impossible.

God loves us, and in His ultimate wisdom, He speaks to us, holds our hand, and leads us to a path that brings us more blessings, peace, joy, and love than we could ever dream.

The path may not be easy, but it so exceeds our dreams and expectations that we immediately know it is God's hand at work opening and closing doors.

> We know that in everything God works for good with those who love him, who are called according to His purpose. (Romans 8:28)

Thanks be to God.
Amen.

RECIPE FOR LIFE

A recipe gives us directions to follow to get the best results when cooking or baking.

One measures the amount for each ingredient. And then adds them together and mixes or stirs according to the recipe. The best part is the final product when it is ready to eat or taste. It is the best until one day you taste someone else's recipe. It may have a special ingredient that makes it better than yours.

In some ways, our life is like a recipe. We follow a plan that we create for our life and believe it will all work out. However, plans change, things happen, life intervenes, and then one has to alter the recipe, for better or for worse.

> For I know the plans I have for you says the Lord, plans for welfare and not evil, to give you a future and a hope. (Jeremiah 29:11)

> He has showed you, O man, what is good; and what does the Lord require of you but to do justice, to love kindness, and to walk humbly with your God? (Micah 6:8)

God gives us Jesus, His Son, as an example to follow. God gives us His word, the Bible, which contains instructions on how to act, how to worship, and what is acceptable and what is not. God gives us the Holy Spirit and prayer so He can talk to us and we can talk to Him at any time. God shows us the way to an abundant life with Him; it is up to us to choose to follow or not.

When we follow Jesus, we study His word and the scripture. He fills us with His wisdom and knowledge. He also equips us for the work He has for us to do (2 Timothy 3:16–17). As we meditate on God's word and begin to understand it with His help, we allow Him to show us His way (Joshua 1:8). As we listen and obey God, we choose His way and will over our own (Acts 5:29).

God gives us the Bible, His scripture, our recipe for life. The Bible speaks to us and shows us God's recipe to a better path. We don't need to change God, His ingredients or His ways. His way is the best and only way to abound in love, mercy, grace, and life. Come, follow Jesus, He is the way to abundant life. A life that is full of love, forgiveness, and blessings. God's way is the best recipe for life.

Thanks be to God.

Amen.

RETURN TO THE LORD

> Therefore, say to them, Thus says the Lord
> of hosts; Return to me, says the Lord of hosts,
> and I will return to you, says the Lord of hosts.
> (Zechariah 1:3)

> Rend your hearts and not your clothing. Return
> to the Lord, your God, for He is gracious and
> merciful, slow to anger, and abounding in stead-
> fast love, and relents from punishing. (Joel 2:13)

> I will give them a heart to know that I am the
> Lord; and they shall be my people and I will be
> their God, for they shall return to me with their
> whole heart. (Jeremiah 24:7)

A child runs away from her mother in anger and runs to her room
and slams the door. Older children try to run away from home when
they become angry. They believe they can manage everything on their
own. They do not want help from anyone. Soon they find out they
need help either from their parents or from someone else. They end
up returning home or to a place of shelter. They discover this world
is not a friendly place and we all need help in one way or another.

As we walk through life, we stumble and fall. We mess up. We
do or say things out of anger. We do the things we don't want to do.

We treat others badly, we swear, we cheat, and we lie. Sometimes we don't even know we are doing these things. We think we don't need God and we can do things all on our own. We seek our own earthly desires.

We run away from the one true God, who will always welcome us, love us, forgive us, and pardon us from all our sins, our messing up, and even our false thinking that we can live without Him.

God loves us so much, He never will leave us. He is always calling and searching for His lost children. God is our hope and our help. Return to Him. God fights for us and meets us where we are at and encourages us and helps us to return to Him. God sees us and the desires of our heart. So when we become unable to love Him or come to Him, He intervenes for us and helps us return to Him. God, the Good Shepherd, is always looking and calling for His lost sheep. Return to God. His love and salvation is always there waiting for you and for me.

Return to God, our father, maker, redeemer, and friend.

Thanks be to God.

Amen.

IDLENESS

Behold, this was the guilt of you sister Sodom; she and her daughters had pride, surfeit of food, and prosperous ease, but did not aid the poor and needy. (Ezekiel 16:49)

A slack hand causes poverty, but the hand of the diligent make us rich. (Proverbs 10:4)

And we desire each one of you to show the same earnestness in realizing the full assurance of hope till the end, so that you may not be sluggish, but imitators of those who through faith and patience inherit the promises. (Hebrews 6:11–12)

Idleness is more than being a couch potato or sitting while playing video games all day. Idleness in the Bible is about being sluggish or lazy in our commitment to Jesus and in our service, love, and trust in Him. If our heart and mind are not on God, we become idle. Being idle or lazy gives Satan an opportunity to come in with His worldly thoughts and desires. He can overtake us and lead us away from God to selfishness, self-indulgence, and soon self-destruction.

Idleness affects not only our own life, but also the life of others around us. Our light does not shine for Jesus but for ourselves.

We end up avoiding things we should be doing with the things we should not be doing.

Idleness can lead to sin, which is not of God. So the more we become attentive to Jesus, seek Him and His forgiveness, we keep idleness at bay. We keep our focus on Jesus with His help by serving Him, sharing His saving grace, encouraging one another in love, and telling others of His love.

Be alert, watch and pray, keep our heart, mind, and soul on Him, then we keep idleness and sinfulness away.

Thanks be to God.

Amen.

JUNCTIONS: WHICH WAY TO GO

Thou dost show me the path of life, in thy presence there is fullness of joy, in thy right hand are pleasures for ever more. (Psalm 16:11)

Teach me they way, O Lord, that I may walk in thy truth; unite my heart to fear thy name. (Psalm 86:11)

Trust in the Lord with all your heart, and do not rely on your own insight. In all your ways acknowledge him, and he will make straight your paths. (Proverbs 3:5–6)

As we travel on the roads around the country, we run into many forks and junctions in the road. How do we determine which way to go? Because we certainly will not ask for directions! But now with cell phones and navigation systems on board our vehicles, we are able to Google directions at any time.

In our life, there is always a different road or path to take. We don't know which path to take, but we need to make a decision. We don't need Google or a map, but we do need God in our life to help us. We need to be in a relationship with Him because we need His help. We need to talk to Him, and He needs to talk to us. God will always give us the right directions for our life; He is never wrong. Obstacles and challenges always crop up along the way, but He is always with us to help guide and direct us on the right path. We need to trust, believe, and have faith in Him and obey Him because He does have our best interest at heart. So we pray and listen to Him, then we make the best decision possible with His guidance and wisdom. As God leads our steps, He shines His light on the right path for us. If we falter or get lost, His light is always there for us, shining on the path that leads back to Him.

There is always a junction on the road of life; one way leads us nearer to God, to His help, wisdom, and love; the other way leads us further away from God, toward selfishness, frustration, and fear.

God is always calling and waiting for us to follow Him. He is always willing to lead us to the path that is best for us and to the way that leads to Him—to truth, to peace, to love, and to an abundant life. It is our choice.

When junctions come into our life, follow Him, for He is the way to truth, light, and life.

Thanks be to God.

Amen.

CLUTTER AND BURDENS

Cast your burdens on the Lord, He will sustain you; He will never permit the righteous to be moved. (Psalm 55:22)

Come to me, all who labor and are heavy laden, and I will give you rest. Take my yoke upon you, and learn from me; for I am gentle and lowly in heart, and you will find rest for you souls. (Matthew 11:28–29)

Cast all your anxieties on Him, for He cares for you. (1 Peter 5:7)

In my house, a room and a few drawers become my clutter places. The clutter takes up space and is an untidy mess. The clutter creates chaos and becomes indicative of my life at times. The clutter and chaos make it almost impossible to move around it or even move beyond it. In our lives, we hold on to clutter, turmoil, and litter—stuff we do not need. When we hold on to it, we end up getting stuck and not being able to move on or forward because of the mess.

God tells us to take our burdens, our clutter, our turmoil, our struggles, our sorrows, our losses, our fears, our messes, and our anxieties and lay them at the foot of the cross. We need to U-Haul all the unnecessary stuff that drag us down and mess up our lives, and we need to give it away; give it to Jesus. He wants us to surrender all our burdens and stresses to Him and allow Him to carry the load. Jesus takes away our fears, worries, and burdens. Let Him renew, restore, and give us peace and rest. Trust and believe in Him, allow Jesus to work and to provide for our every need.

Come, listen and hear God's words and promises. Allow Him to love, care, and sustain us. Call on God, allow Him to love, care, sustain, and give our troubled spirit peace and rest from the clutter and burdens of the day.

Thanks be to God.

Amen.

WONDERS

Heavens are telling the glory of God and the fir-
mament proclaim His handiwork. (Psalm 19:1)

O Lord, thou art my God; I will exalt thee, I will
praise thy name; for thou hast done wonderful
things, plans formed of old, faithful and sure.
(Isaiah 25:1)

The seven wonders of the ancient world, according to Wikipedia,
are the most spectacular wonders and man-made structures in the
world. The only ancient wonder that still exists is the Great Pyramids
of Giza.

The creation of the sunrise or the sunset is a spectacular wonder, along with the aurora borealis. I believe the sunrise and sunset
may be a glimpse of what a wondrous home in heaven awaits us, as
His children. He proclaims His love for us in and through His many
wonders. There is beauty, majesty, and power in every changing pan-
orama of sunrise or sunset.

God and His creation is beyond our human comprehension.
He is able to communicate to us without words. He shows His power
and wisdom through the wonders of the sunrise and sunset and leads

us to glorify and praise His name. There is joy, peace, and hope in the wonders of His creation.

> So that those who dwell at earth's farthest bounds are afraid at thy signs; thou markest the outgo-ings of the morning and the evening to shout for joy. (Psalm 65:8)

The whole earth is filled with God's wonder. Praise His holy name.

Thanks be to God.

Amen.

GOD SPEAKS THE TRUTH

God speaks the truth. God speaks to our heart, our soul, and our mind in love. God speaks, and the heavens open, and the glory and the love of God abounds for you and for me.

Loving God, helps us be aware and sensitive to Your voice when You call and speak to us. Help us to listen and receive Your message in our heart, soul, and mind. Thank You for speaking to us in truth and in love. Thank You for your steadfast love, mercy, and faithfulness. Help us to listen, hear, believe, trust, and obey when You speak. Thank You for being our God—a God of love, grace, forgiveness, and hope.

Thanks be to God.

Amen.

SECTION 4

Living Our Life for Christ

LIVE IN AND FOR CHRIST

God sent His Son Jesus to the world to save us from our sin and to show us another way to live. When we decide to live in and for Christ, we allow Christ to enter our life as our Savior and Lord. We decide to put our life and our hope in His hands, to trust and believe in Christ. We also want to know everything possible about our God. So we study and read His word, listen to His voice, worship and praise Him, learn from fellow believers and their experiences.

As we grow and develop our faith, knowledge, and trust in Him, our heart changes.

We become a new creation in Christ, and our old sinful self falls away. Our life becomes about Christ in us, helping us and showing us how to love our neighbor, building one another up, encouraging one another, and putting others first. As followers of Christ, we love, serve, show kindness, care for others, give of ourselves with selflessness and humility. God's love abounds in us and through us to show others His mercy, grace, forgiveness, and hope for all. God's light in us shines for others to see and to know the love of God is for them as well.

Even though we live in Christ, we still struggle. We struggle with our self, sin, and trusting Him. However, in those struggles, Christ is always with us and helping us through it all. He supplies all our needs, abides with us, walks with us, guards us, protects us, and surrounds us with love and strength to endure and bring us through our struggles and trials. Through every experience, we learn to trust God in and with everything. With God, all things are possible.

God's work is never done. His work in us is never done, and our work is never done. It is a process of learning, growing, and developing in trust and faith in God.

As we follow in His footsteps, we learn more about His love and truths. He transforms our heart, soul, and mind; and we begin to live in His love and forgiveness from that day forward.

When we live in Christ, we become God's hands and feet in this world. We become the face of Jesus for others. God's love shines through our actions and deeds. Others see God's light in our heart, through our selflessness, our humility, and through our serving, and they want to know where such love and kindness come from.

May these meditations, talks, prayers, and insights be a blessing to you.

A TREE

He is like a tree planted by streams of water, that yield fruit in its season, and its leaf does not wither. (Psalm 1:3)

Trees live all around us. Trees have trunks that provide support for the tree and transport food and material to other parts of the tree. Tree trunks grow and search for light to help them grow. We too have trunks or a core that can be strong or weak, straight or curved due to stresses of life. We too are also searching for the light.

A tree spreads out its roots in the ground and anchors the tree. The roots extract nutrients and moisture from the soil for growth. Just as a root for tree is necessary, a family tree and many of its traditions is also important. However, the roots we grow in Christ is our most important anchor. Grounded in Christ, we draw on His love, truths, and promises. Then when the wind blows, we stand firm and secure in Christ.

Tree branches need pruning due to overgrowth, dead areas caused by aphids or fungus that can spread if not removed, and the tree dies. So pruning stimulates new growth and fruit and a healthy and stable productive tree. We too need pruning, pruning of those undesirable thoughts, false thinking, and our leftover baggage. If no pruning occurs, these things weigh us down and shape us into something we do not want to be. When we just rely on ourselves to provide our daily needs for life, we sway to and fro in the wind and become unstable and displaced due to our shallow roots.

As Christ as our anchor, we have a source of living water, life, and light where love, mercy, grace, truth, and forgiveness abound. Christ takes away our sin, guilt, our extra baggage, and transforms us into new creations. When we live as new creations, grounded and anchored in Christ, we stand strong and steadfast in His love in spite of the storms, wind, sickness, and stress.

We stand firm in Christ, gathering His truths, ways, and light to grow and bear good fruit, as a tree planted by the stream of living water.

Thanks be to God.

Amen.

LOVE IS PATIENT

The dictionary defines *patience* as "bearing pain or suffering calmly or without complaint."

It is hard to endure suffering with calmness. It is hard to ask and let others help you. It is difficult to slow down, rest, and heal and let God renew, supply, and lead us to a new way of thinking and acting. Patience is one of those attributes you cannot learn by reading about it. It requires one to endure a situation and actively work on being patient.

Traffic frustrates everyone. Being stuck in traffic or dealing with rude drivers creates an opportunity for us to work on being patient, calming down, and being content at the time.

Remember 1 Corinthians 13:4, "LOVE IS PATIENT."

We all need patience. Patience is a gift from God. It is good for our health, our life, and others. God loves us and wants the best for us. We need to set our minds on the things of Christ and His example of what patience is. When we set our minds on being more patient, life presents itself with more opportunities to be patient. Instead of becoming frustrated and upset, we trust in God and submit to His will and listen to Him and allow His patience to work in and through us. When we do this, we end up ministering in a special way to others. They see patience and calmness, God's good work in us.

The Lord teaches us about a more perfect love, that is, patience, and that moves us to be more Christlike. When we show more Christlike patience in our actions and deeds, others see and feel from us that "love is patient." They also witness a transformation, and they too become transformed by God's love.

Love is patient. Allow God's patience, love, and light to shine in and through us.

Thanks be to God.

Amen.

Walking with God

Enoch walked with God. (Genesis 5:22–24)

Sounds easy, but walking with God is easier said than done.

We try to walk with God, but many times we find ourselves tiptoeing around trying to hide or avoiding God's voice or making up an excuse not to do what he asks. Other times we find ourselves tripping over our own feet, trying with all our might to keep up the pace, but at other times we just get distracted by other stuff. Only once in a while do we find ourselves in step with God, walking the same direction, letting God be in control of our life, listening to Him, and obeying when He calls. But when we walk with God, His strength, power, and light shines through us to others.

God makes us a new creation and gives us a new direction, purpose, and vision. Every day we walk with God, the less we become attached to the things of this world. God protects us from our enemies and gives us a spirit of love, light, wisdom, discernment, and action to be a blessing for others. Walking with God is a journey we take with Him. We walk with Him through faith and trust and only with His help.

God is calling us. Listen to Him. Obey and take action for the Lord.

No more selective hearing or actions.

Take hold of God's hand and walk with Him.

Thanks be to God.

Amen.

WHO IS COUNTING ON WHO?

Is someone counting on you?

Are you counting on God?

Is God counting on you?

God loves each of us and sent his Son to save us and give us life. And He gives us life abundantly. As God's children, we begin a journey of love, service, ministry, hardships, and blessings. It is a journey and ministry that is not done alone. It is best accomplished with God and all His children working together for good and His glory. We put our trust and hope in God, and He puts His trust and hope in us to be His hands and feet in this world, to light and to shine in the darkness.

It is through faith and love in Jesus and through the indwelling of the Holy Spirit that move us to action. Many times our actions speak louder than words. We show love to others as Christ loves us. Then it is possible to live in harmony and peace with one another because of God's love. We show patience and understanding to others. We encourage one another. We forgive one another. We help one another. We show kindness to all. We care for others, and we become a blessing to others by our actions and deeds. We bring *hope*—the hope and love of Christ to those we meet. This is the work and ministry of God to which He calls us and is ever before us.

Show God's love, light, kindness, and goodness to all on our journey and do not defer or neglect it, for we may not pass that way again.

> For as the body apart from the spirit is dead, so
> faith apart from works is dead. (James 2:26)

We trust God, show love, do good, and give hope—by the power of the Holy Spirit within us. The ministry and mission of God is ever before each of us. Go with God.

Thanks be to God.

Amen.

LIVE FOR CHRIST

No one can serve two masters; for either he will hate the one and love the other, or he will be devoted to the one and despise the other. You cannot serve God and mammon. (Matthew 6:24)

And He died for all, that those who live might live no longer for themselves but for Him, who for their sake died and was raised. (2 Corinthians 5:15)

I say to myself, "I got this. I am in control today. I am positive, I got this. Life is good today. No problems today." Some days I feel like this, but most of the time, I am just trying to survive.

Life is a balancing act between a job, children, spouse, and taking care of the house. It is a balancing act between living life the way I want and living life the way God wants me to. It's a balancing act between living a life that is not too good and not too bad. It is living a life with just enough good works, just a little gossip, and a little idolatry, but not too much of one thing or another. This is life trying to serve two masters. It is also known as sitting on a fence. This leads to a life of frustration, struggles, and inner conflict. Trying to serve two masters, God and self, is impossible because they are in conflict most of the time. God says one way or the other, no partway, and no sitting on the fence.

> Set your mind on things above, not on things that are on earth. (Colossians 3:2)

> To set your mind on flesh is death, but to set the mind on the spirit is life and peace. (Romans 8:6)

God says we cannot have it both ways. When we believe and trust in Him, it is all or nothing. If we focus on all worldly things, it is certain death. When we set our mind and heart on Christ, there is life and peace. When we let the never weary Holy Spirit work in us, God becomes the center of our life, and we have a new life. His abiding love, forgiveness, strength, and power makes all things possible. The old nature passes away, and we become a new creation in Christ; our attitude and actions then change. When God is the center of our life, we don't have to solve all the issues by ourselves. The balancing act ends because of God. Struggles and pain still occur, but God is always with us to help and to provide strength for us in all situations. His love is always with us and it is unending.

God is waiting; seek Him, trust in His words and promises. No matter what happens, in life or in death, we are His. He is always with us to help us through all circumstances. Live in Christ.

Thanks be to God.

Amen.

WORKERS IN THE KINGDOM OF GOD

Greet Prisca and Aquilla, my fellow workers in
Christ Jesus. (Romans 16:3)

For we are fellow workers for God; you are God's
field, God's building. (1 Corinthians 3:9)

God welcomes each of us into the family of God, when we accept
Jesus as our Savior and Lord. We become members of the body of
Christ and become a worker in the family of God, the body of Christ.
Each of us has a job, a skill, and a gift from God, either known or
known, for the uplifting and encouragement of others and to build
up the family of God. God relies on us to share His love, the Gospel,
our gifts, and to be His hands and feet in this world. We rely on Him,
the source of our strength, endurance, motivation, and direction for
our life to step out in faith to share the love of God to all.

All of us, God and His people, join together to serve a risen
Lord and to build up the family of God. We trust God to supply all
our needs for our journey as we step out in faith. He calls each of us
to minister in the place we are in or in a new place or in an unex-
pected place or somewhere with new responsibilities. He helps us to
share our faith with others and to fellowship with all people in His
name.

God promises that if we do not quit, we shall reap benefits if we do not lose heart. Let us continue the work God calls us to do. Help us love, serve, and plant the word of God wherever we may be.

As workers in His kingdom, let our good works, deeds, actions, and love build one another up to the honor and glory of God.

Thanks be to God.

Amen.

Power of God
Working In One Life

> He is like a tree planted by streams of water, that yields its fruit in its season and its leaf does not wither. In all that he does, he prospers. (Psalm 1:3)

> Either make the tree good, and its fruit good; or make the tree bad, and its fruit bad; for the tree is known by its fruit. (Matthew 12:33)

There is beauty and power in a single tree sprouting among the rocks. There is beauty and power in the one and only tree on the side of the hill growing straight and tall with no other vegetation around.

The nurturing and powerful word of God fills us and radiates through us so that we become like the tree that grows tall in and amongst the rocks for all to see. We proclaim God's word and love even in desolate places and become the tree of life for those in that particular place. When we declare God's love to a world of confusion, despair, and loneliness, others see Jesus and His love in us and believe. So if He can change one life, then He certainly can change others.

The power of God can change a life, and He uses one life to change others.

Thanks be to God.

Amen.

POWER OF GOD'S PATH

Teach me thy way, O Lord; and lead me on a level path because of my enemies. (Psalm 27:11)

For the gate is narrow and the way is hard, that leads to life, and those who find it are few. (Matthew 7:14)

To give Light to those who sit in darkness and in shadows of death, to guide our feet into the way of peace. (Luke 1:79)

One often hears the following: "I can find it." or "I don't need help." or "I don't need a map." or "I am certainly not going to ask anyone for directions." The road of life is long; it has many curves and exits, and it gets windy and bumpy. The roads can be hazardous, so we end up following someone or pulling over to the side of the road or traveling slowly. It is easy to get lost and wander aimlessly looking for the road because of the many signs and directions. Still, we think we don't need help because "we got this."

In life, our path or calling is difficult. So instead of dealing with all of it ourselves, we need to let go and let God. It is time to let go of our pride and selfishness and call on God for help. The difficult roads, trials, struggles, and callings to difficult places and situations become challenging. Let God help, guide, and direct us back onto the right path. The road becomes easier when we believe and trust in God to help and light the way. He is always with us, walks with us, and helps us as we go forth with Him, traveling the road less traveled, to a new path. A path that leads us to a better way and to a better life is life with God. When we walk by faith, we walk in God's love and power to guide and direct our steps to a life with meaning and purpose in Him.

Walk with God. Allow Him to guide and direct us to a life of love, truth, and light in Christ.

Thanks be to God.

Amen.

DOERS OF THE WORD

But be doers of the Word and not hearers only,
deceiving yourselves. (James 1:22)

If you know these things, blessed are you if you
do them. (John 13:17)

Stand up, follow God, do what is right, and do what needs to be done.

There is a difference between hearing and doing.

God calls each of us to be doers of His word.

God calls us into action. Every child of God is expected to act and do something positive in and for the mission and ministry of God. But, everyone is different, and, therefore, their gift and action is different. But each person is to respond according to their gifts, desires, and willingness to do God's work.

As a child of God, we are set free from sin and slavery by the blood of Jesus, according to Galatians 5:1. But it is still our choice, whether to be a doer of the word or just a hearer.

If we decide to be a doer of the word, we ask God to help us put away our excuses, our sinfulness, our selfishness, and ask for help to stop blaming others for our inactivity. We ask God to forgive us and help us to step out of our safe environment, into action and be a doer of the Word.

It is time to listen and to trust God to help us respond to His call. It is time to take a risk, step out in faith, and be a doer of the word with God's help.

It is time to share and use the gifts from God for others and for good. It is time to share the good news of Christ and share our clothes and food to those in need. It is time to seek the Lord for knowledge, wisdom, and discernment and share the love of Christ to everyone.

God calls us to be doers of the word. So out of a Spirit-led heart and mind, we too love and bless others as Christ loves and blesses us.

Thanks be to God.

Amen.

PINE CONES

That Christ may dwell in your hearts through faith, that you, being rooted and grounded in love may have power to comprehend with all the saints what is the breadth and length and height and depth and to know the love of Christ which surpasses knowledge, that you may be filled with all the fullness of God. (Ephesians 3:17–19)

As, therefore, you received Christ Jesus the Lord, so live in him, rooted and built up in him, and established in the faith, just as you were taught, abounding in thanksgiving. (Colossians 2:6–7)

We live where pine trees abound. The pine trees drop their cones everywhere. And the squirrels hide them in and under everything. We seem to be constantly picking them up, out of every nook and cranny. No matter what we do to get rid of the cones before the seeds mature, there are still hundreds of seedlings growing every spring in the yard and rock garden.

The pine cones grow while still connected and rooted in the tree. When the pine cones mature, they release their seeds, and they fall and take root in the soil of the garden or yard, not more than ninety feet away from the mother tree. As it turns out, the mother tree and other trees around it, together, provide an underground network of roots that increase the seedling chance of survival in that soil.

Rooted in Christ, we live in His word, love, salvation, and forgiveness. We stay close to our source of love, strength, peace, and comfort, which is Jesus Christ. When we stray too far away from Christ, we become fragile and vulnerable. We lose our source of life, light, and strength. We too, like the pine tree, do not grow well or stand tall when we wander too far from our source, Jesus. We need Jesus, who is our light and life. We depend, trust, rely on Him to always be with us and help us. Rooted in Christ and in the word, we grow in faith and learn to trust in His word, promises.

Being rooted in Christ—who is our source of love, strength, salvation, forgiveness, and light—we become a blessing to others. Just as Christ shows us love, kindness, and help, we too show others the same love and kindness.

Be rooted in Christ, in His love and in His word, to be His light in a world of darkness.

Thanks be to God.

Amen.

LIVING IN CHRIST

Life is worth living only when we become new creations in Christ. It is through God's love, mercy, and grace that meaning and purpose are given to our life, and it becomes full and complete.

We live in Christ, and we follow His example through God's grace and power. He transforms our heart and mind and calls us to live a new life by the power of the Holy Spirit.

> Then let us no more pass judgment on one another, but rather decide never to put a stumbling block or hindrance in the way of a brother. (Romans 14:13)

> Let us pursue what makes for peace and for mutual up building. (Romans 14:19)

> May the God of steadfastness and encouragement grant you to live in such harmony with one another, in accordance with Christ Jesus, that together you may with one voice glorify the God and Father of our Lord Jesus Christ. (Romans 15:5–6)

He calls us to live a new life in Christ.

This causes us to pray constantly, to help one another with brotherly love, to show patience and kindness in all circumstances, to live in harmony with all, and not to show others evil for evil, but overcome evil with good.

We show compassion to others. We build one another up and encourage one another.

We live unto the Lord and glorify His holy name.

As we each live in Christ, He fills each of us with faith, joy, peace, and love to give and share with others.

Thanks be to God.

Amen.

LIVE IN HOPE

Life is unbearable, depressing, hurtful, and is filled with many problems.

Take heart—listen to the still small voice of the Holy Spirit within you.

God loves you and will take care of you. With the Lord, there is love and redemption. According to a certain hymn, "Our hope is built on nothing less than Jesus's blood and righteousness." Instead of losing all hope, immerse yourself in God's word.

As in Romans 15:4, which says, "For whatever was written in the former days was written for our instruction, that by the steadfastness and by the encouragement of the scriptures we may have Hope."

> The God of Hope fill you with all joy and peace
> in believing, so that by the power of the Holy
> Spirit you may abound in hope. (Romans 15:13)

So when those long nights come with doubts, fear, worry, and anxiety, turn to God. Turn to His word and promises. He is always with us, through all our struggles, and He provide us with comfort, peace, and calmness.

Even though we cannot see the indwelling of the Holy Spirit or God's forgiveness or God's resurrection or His promises of eternal life, we believe through faith. And this is the faith and hope we live in Jesus.

He fills us with His faith, hope, and truth.

He fills us with His word and love, which is boundless and everlasting.

Live in the hope of Jesus

Live according to His words and promises.

Live in hope and expectation of eternal life with Him.

Thanks be to God.

Amen.

LAMENTING

Sometimes the road of life is long and winding, and we just want to get off the road for a while, shut everything off and everyone out. We need a break from moaning and groaning, crying and sobbing. Enough is enough.

In the Bible, *lamenting* is the word they use for "moaning and groaning." Psalms 31 and 77 are lamenting psalms; they give words to our feelings and emotional state and help us talk to God.

When we turn to God, He hears us and responds with open arms and love. He listens and reminds us of His promises and blessings. Remember, He led the Israelites through the sea, He works wonders, and He redeems His people. Remember, He blesses His people. His goodness abounds for those who love Him. Even today, He continues to show His love for us and never forgets or leaves us.

God hears our moaning, groaning, and sighing and comes to us to reassure us of His love. Then we, in turn, praise God for His steadfast love and live in that knowledge, which gives hope, comfort, and strength. Life happens, and God doesn't promise us a "rose garden" where life is perfect. God is with us and suffers everything we suffer, so He understands us and meets us where we are at and provides us with His love and promises. He allows us to suffer and to go through our struggles to learn, to grow, and to move forward. He is always with us and holds on to us, leading us and surrounding us with His arms and love. He carries us through the storms.

There is no particular pattern or pat answer in the Bible for a solution to a situation or to an issue. One verse is not the answer; we need to dwell and abide in the steadfast and unchanging word and love of God. God loves us and allows us to go through the valley and helps us reach the other side. With God, our life is hopeful, joyful, peaceful, good, and above all, full of the life-changing love of God.

God loves us and is always with us. He hears and answer us and helps us through all circumstances.

Praise and thanks be to God.

Amen.

WINDMILLS

We have seen many windmills in many states on road trips. They line the roads, hills, and the rivers. They stand tall against the sky. The large blades go around by the force of the wind, turning the wind into energy. Energy that is stored, to be used at a later time.

Sometimes we feel like windmills. We stand tall and fast with God. Our hearts and minds go round and round, searching and gathering information and storing up knowledge and wisdom about Jesus from the scriptures and fellow Christians. We learn and read God's Word, we worship, we pray, and we fellowship, in order to gather all we can about God's love and mercy. We store it up for ourselves—in our heart, mind, and soul.

> For as the body apart from the spirit is dead, so
> faith apart from works is dead. (James 2:26)
>
> If we live by the spirit, let us walk by the Spirit.
> (Galatians 5:25)

So God says what good is it if we store information, knowledge, and wisdom but do nothing with it. It just sits unused and useless. So let us call on God for help to use the gifts given, to be a blessing to others. Let Him help us and give us what we need for our journey, whether it is energy, power, strength, endurance, patience, peace, or wisdom. Whatever the need be, it is ours. God says ask in His name and receive. So ask Him in faith, and He supplies all our needs as we step out in faith with fearlessness and determination to continue God's ministry of spreading God's love to all.

God is ready and willing and waiting to help us step out in faith. We become His hands and feet, His light, and His servant in a world in need.

The blades turn, filling us up with the love of God; it is overflowing within each of us. So let the love, trust, and faith in Jesus overflow into our words, actions, deeds, and good works to show others of God's everlasting love.

Thanks be to God.

Amen.

CHURCH SIGN

I recently came across this church signboard:

> NO GOD
> NO HOPE
> KNOW GOD
> KNOW HOPE

I have thought a lot about what the sign said. We struggle with many things in our life. We struggle to pay debts, we struggle with fear as the world continues to be in turmoil, or we struggle when the money only goes so far. And when we struggle, we get depressed as soon as disappointments arise. Seek God and His promises. God is enough. He is the only one with the help and answers that we need. He is the only one that will stand with us through our struggles.

> And now, Lord, for what do I wait? My hope is in thee. (Psalm 39:7)

> For whatever was written in former days was written for our instruction, that by steadfastness and by encouragement of scriptures we might have hope. (Romans 15:4)

For I know the plans I have for you says the Lord,
plans for welfare and not evil, to give you a future
and a hope. (1 Corinthians 15:19)

God claims us as His children. He loves each of us and will take care of us no matter what, and that is His promise to us. God is enough.

He is our Savior and Lord, He is our peace, and He is our joy and hope.

He gives and supplies us with everything we need.

Deep in my heart and in the heart of all His children, He plants and grows His love and word, and no one can take that away. Our hope is in God. Rely on Him, believe in Him, and trust in Him for all things. God is from everlasting to everlasting.

KNOW GOD, KNOW HOPE.

GOD IS ENOUGH.

Thanks be to God.

Amen.

EQUIPPED

(God gives gifts), "for the equipment of saints, for the work of ministry, for building up the body of Christ." (Ephesians 4:12)

And God is able to provide you with every blessing in abundance, so that you may always have enough of everything and may provide in abundance for every good work. (2 Corinthians 9:8)

We love and serve the Lord. In our service, we are to be diligent in our worship and in our financial commitment to Him. As we listen to God, we let His voice and light lead us. But many times we feel ill-equipped for life, and at other times, we feel we have everything we need for our journey. God promises to be with us and provide all we need for our journey. He provides us with mercy, love, grace, and forgiveness. He equips us, strengthens us, empowers us, loves us, watches over us, feeds us, and clothes us. He forgives us, encourages us, grants us mercy and grace, and blesses us beyond anything we could ask or think.

Christ and His love is always there for us. We can do all these things and more because of Jesus Christ. Nothing is impossible with God.

God is calling. Listen, step out in faith, trust in his promises, obey and serve Him—in all things.

God calls and equips us, as His disciples, to be His hands and feet to a world in need and to build up the body of Christ. He lifts us up and helps us through all situations. God equips us so that we always have enough. Go, trust, and believe in Him and His word that equips us for service.

Thanks be to God. Amen.

CHOOSE

We have a few remote-controlled cars around the house. Everyone loves to play with them, especially the grandchildren. Remote control cars require a control box with buttons on it to make it go forward, backward, stop, reverse, move to the right and the left. Then one needs batteries for the control box and someone to work the controls, or the car does nothing.

God is not our controller or the person using a control box.

God is our Father, our Lord, and our Savior. He is steadfast and faithful to His people. God provides guidance and direction with love.

God is not making us do that or this.

We are a people of free will. We make our own choices.

We choose to follow and obey God or not.

We choose the road less traveled or not.

We choose to love our neighbors or not.

We choose to give of our time and talent or not.

We choose.

We choose, but we have to live with the result or outcome of those choices.

> And if you be unwilling to serve the Lord, choose
> this day whom you will serve, whether the gods
> your fathers served in the region beyond the river,
> or the gods of the Amorites in whose land you

dwell; but for me and my house, we will serve the Lord. (Joshua 24:15)

God came into the world to be our God and Father and to send His Son to save us from our sins, to become our Savior and Lord. God loves us so much that He comes to provide us—a sinful people—a way to have life, and have it abundantly with Him. God loves us. We are His children. We are His people. He saves us, but He cannot make us believe or follow Him. It is our choice. Just like the people in the Bible, many people believed in Him and many others did not.

It is our free will to choose to trust, believe, and obey Him.

And it is because of Christ and His love, we seek, ask, and desire a new life. A new way to think, live, and act.

Create in me a clean heart, O God, and put a new and right spirit within me. Cast me not a way from thy presence, and take not thy Holy Spirit from me. Restore to me the joy of they salvation, and uphold me with a willing spirit. (Psalm 51:10–12)

We choose Christ and His Word to dwell within us so that whatever we do in word and deed, we do in the name of the Lord and to glorify Him.

Thanks be to God. Amen.

STRUGGLES

When the cares of my heart are many, thy consolations cheer my soul. (Psalm 94:19)

Fear not, for I am with you, be not dismayed, for I am your God; I will strengthen you, I will help you, I will uphold you with my victorious right hand. (Isaiah 41:10)

Rejoice in your hope, be patient in tribulation, be constant in prayer. (Romans 12:12)

We all struggle. We struggle with life because things in life seem to be constantly changing or because things happen we can't control or don't expect. We struggle with decisions, relationships, money, finances, and we even struggle with our faith.

Sometimes it seems that we struggle with our struggling.

God calls us to take all our struggles, our fears, our anger, our frustrations, our anxieties, our worries—anything and everything to the foot of the cross. We give them all to Jesus and leave them there. Let go of all of it and let Jesus carry the load.

And we trust in Jesus's words and promises. He takes care of all things. He is always with us, and He always helps us through any and all situations. He supplies our every need. He brings His hope, peace, comfort, and strength to our struggling heart, mind, and soul. He renews our spirit and gives us strength, endurance, encouragement, and patience during our struggles.

When we pray and ask God for His help, He answers. He is in the midst of our struggles, in the midst of things we do not understand, and in the midst of change. He guides and directs our steps through our struggles and helps provides us with a way through our problem as we trust and rely on Him.

Lord, we come to You for guidance in all that we do and say. In the midst of our struggles and in the midst of change, guide and direct our steps and lead us on the right path. A path that leads to love, peace, comfort, and hope in You.

Give us your peace, courage, and wisdom to go forth, trusting in You for all things.

Thanks be to God.

Amen.

SPIRITUAL STRENGTH

According to the label on the Colgate Total toothpaste box, "Brushing teeth with this product makes teeth clean and white. It also protects the teeth against tartar and gum disease and the enamel is restored and made strong."

We brush our teeth to protect them and make them strong so they last a long time.

> Put on the whole armor of God that we may
> be able to stand against the wiles of the devil.
> (Ephesians 6:11)

Ephesians 6:13–20 says that we are to surround and secure ourselves with truth on which all else is built upon, God's truth. We are to put on the breastplate of righteousness, shod our feet with equipment of the Gospel of peace, put on the shield of faith, the helmet of salvation, the sword of the Spirit, which is the word of God, and to pray at all times.

We need to protect and strengthen our spiritual life as well as our physical body. We need to protect our spiritual life against evil, wickedness, darkness, or anything that will separate us from God. We put on the whole suit of armor of God, not part, but all, to protect us and to stand firm with God against evil. We put on Christ—His truth, righteousness, peace, salvation, faith, and the word of the

Lord. And we pray at all times to stand with God against the seen and unseen enemies in this world.

The armor of God, His strength and courage, the Holy Spirit, faith, trust, and perseverance become necessary to withstand the attacks of evil and darkness on various fronts and strategies. Satan uses trickery and deception—anything to mess with us and trip us up. When we stand fast with God, we do not yield to Satan and the power of evil. Then Satan flees, and we live in the fullness of Christ. God wins the battle, the glory, and the honor.

> Be strong in the Lord and in the strength of His might. (Ephesians 6:10)

Thanks be to God.
Amen.

STORAGE

Farmers store their grain in grain bins or tanks. I store my stuff in drawers, closets, in extra rooms in the basement, in the garage, or in a shed. There are separate storage places for boats and campers. Computer information storage is in a cloud or on a flash drive. Banks store money in vaults. We tend to store our stuff.

God has something to say about storing our treasures.

> Do not store up treasures on earth, where moths and vermin destroy, and where thieves break in and steal, but lay up for yourselves treasures in heaven, where moths and vermin do not destroy and where thieves do no break in and steal. For where your treasure is, there you heart will be also. (Matthew 6:19–21)

We spend our money on what is most important to us. Possessions and money can corrupt and change our heart. We can become selfish and greedy. So we need to be careful of what we own and purchase and what we value.

When we believe and trust in Jesus and put Him first, our heart changes. We seek to increase our faith, love, wisdom, knowledge and seek to be more Christlike. We desire to show love and kindness to all people. We want to serve others. We want to be generous, humble, and a blessing to others.

So it comes down to our heart, our attitude. Are we glorifying ourselves, or are we glorifying God? Greed and selfishness become deceiving and pull us away from the love and forgiveness of our Lord and Savior.

When we live in Jesus, He helps us to be His heart and mind to all people. He helps us show His love and kindness, generosity, helpfulness, and respect to all.

Living in and with Jesus, our attitude and behavior reflect the love of Jesus, and we store up treasures in heaven.

Thanks be to God.

Amen.

THE GREATEST

We all want to be the best or the first or the CEO or the most popular or the greatest. Mohammed Ali proclaimed that he was the greatest.

But Jesus comes and gives new meaning to what it means to be the greatest.

> The greatest among you will be your servant. For those who exalt themselves will be humbled and those who humble themselves will be exalted. (Matthew 23:11)

Jesus becomes our example of what being the greatest and what being a servant in this world is all about. He gives His life for us and for our salvation. He is humble, loving, and kind to all. He helps others and puts their needs first.

When we put God first, He uses those desires in us to be the best or the greatest for His purpose. We become a great witness of His love and forgiveness. We become the best hands and feet of actions and deeds for Christ and to serve Him the best way we can. We bring the good news of Christ to all we meet—with love, excitement, and zeal. We spread the Gospel of Christ with a heart that is humble, generous, selfless, and full of the love of Jesus.

When we love and follow Jesus, we serve Him and think of others first.

Jesus is the greatest, and we honor and glorify Him through our actions, deeds, and in our serving.

Thanks be to God.

Amen.

THE WAY

Make me to know thy ways Lord; teach me thy
paths, lead me in thy truth and teach me, for
thou art the God of my salvation; for thee I wait
all the day long. (Psalm 25:4–5)

All the paths of the Lord are steadfast Love and
Faithfulness, for those who keep His covenant
and His testimonies. (Psalm 25:10)

Let me hear in the morning of thy steadfast love, for
in thee I put my trust. Teach me the way I should
go, for to thee I lift up my soul. (Psalm 143:8)

Yea, thou art my rock and my fortress; for thy
name's sake lead me and guide me. (Psalm 31:3)

A Seeing Eye dog and his owner, a man, walk down the sidewalk.
They seem to be in constant contact with each other. The dog touches
the man's leg ever so slightly, signaling the man to move over, even
though the man has a hold of the leash, which is attached to the dog.
Then the man says something, and the dog nudges the man's leg.
This goes on for a while.

When the man starts to veer off the path, the dog nudges the
man's leg. The man stays on the sidewalk all the way to his destination.

God's hand is always upon us, guiding and directing us in love. God knows each of us personally and only wants the best for us. We choose whether or not to hear, listen, obey, and follow Him.

The Lord is with us, and His love and caring never ends.

Come, hear, listen, believe, and follow Him.

Let Him nudge, guide, and direct our steps in the path He has for us.

Trust in His wisdom, love, might, and word to guide and direct us on the path to a better way and to an abundant life in Jesus Christ.

Walk in the way of the Lord.

Thanks be to God.

Amen.

TUMBLEWEED

Tumbleweed is a plant that dries up and snaps off from its roots and tumbles randomly in the wind. As it tumbles, it randomly gets stuck on a fence, or it gets crushed by a passing car, or it continuously blows about without any direction in the wind.

Sometimes, we as children of God become like tumbleweed. We tumble about here and there with no direction, we get into a situation and get stuck, or we tumble from one belief to another. So when trials and problems arise, and since we have no real convictions or beliefs, we do not know where to go or who to turn to for help. We randomly blow about seeking anyone or anything to help us.

We forget that Jesus is always there for us and He is the answer. He loves us. He is steadfast, faithful, unchangeable, willing to help at any time. He is waiting for us to turn to Him for love, salvation, forgiveness, and help.

> But earnestly desire higher gifts and I will show
> you a more excellent way. (1 Corinthians 12:31)

God is always waiting even when we turn away from Him. The choice is ours.

> But let him ask in faith, with no doubting for he
> who doubts is like wave of the sea that is driven
> and tossed like the wind. (James 1:6)

So we may no longer be children tossed to and fro and carried about with every wind of doctrine, by cunning men, by their craftiness and deceitful wiles. (Ephesians 4:14)

In faith, we ask, receive, and ground ourselves in Jesus Christ. We believe in Him and establish ourselves in His truth, live in His word and in His promises. Christ loves us and equips us for every good work. He supplies all our needs. We stand strong and steadfast in all circumstances with Jesus Christ. He guides and directs us to a better way to the abundant life.

Be grounded in Jesus Christ, stand strong, so as not to be tossed about in the wind when trials come.

Thanks be to God.

Amen.

PEOPLE WATCHING

We watch and observe people daily. We watch and observe others at the park, at the mall, on the street, or in a store. People watching is an American pastime. As we watch and observe others, we begin to judge them. The judgmental comments come from our own prejudices and insecurities. We all become guilty of these comments sooner or later.

When we come to Jesus, in all humility and confessing our sins, we come with all our own faults and issues. God knows of these faults and loves us anyway. He loves and accepts us just the way we are with all our issues. Therefore, we need to accept and love others, but that is only possible when we see them through God's eyes and see the good in them. Judging others is not our job, it belongs to God. God commands us to love others as He loves us.

> This is my commandment that you love one another. (John 15:17)

> Love one another with brotherly affection, outdoing one another in showing honor. (Romans 12:10)

> Be kind to one another, tenderhearted, forgiving one another, just as God in Christ forgave you. (Ephesians 4:32)

When we ask God, in all humility, to forgive our sins, it is through His mercy, grace, and power that He forgives us. And because of His forgiveness, we become righteous before God, and our hearts and minds change. We act differently because of God's forgiveness and love. We forgive, tolerate, and love others because of God and His love for us. We reach out and show love to those around us. We show friendship to all, including the unlovely and the unwanted without judgment. We give support and encouragement to all because of God and His love.

The love of God we show to others transforms them, and in the process, it also transforms us. Love one another as God loves you.

Thanks be to God.

Amen.

DIY, Do It Yourself

Many projects around the house become do-it-yourself projects. There is always something that requires fixing or touching up. Many projects at the office also appear to be do-it-yourself projects. But life itself is difficult, and it is too difficult to be a do-it-yourself project.

> I am the vine, you are the branches. He who abides in me, and I in him, he it is that bears much fruit, for apart from me you can do nothing. (John 15:5)

> I can do anything through Christ who strengthens me. (Philippians 4:13)

> Lord will guide you continually, and satisfy your desire with good things, and make your bones strong. (Isaiah 58:11)

Life is not a DIY project. God did not create us to leave us on this earth to fend for ourselves. When we give our lives over to God, we become children of God. We belong to the Body of Christ. Christ is the head of that body. And He has a plan for each of us as a member of His family.

> For I know the plans I have for you, says the
> Lord, plans for welfare and not evil, to give you a
> future and a hope. (Jeremiah 29:11)

In Jesus, we have life, an abundant life, not just something to endure or get through. It is living a life in Christ, in His love, forgiveness, and hope, and allowing Him to guide and direct our path because He knows, loves, and wants the best for us. He is our future, our strength, our mercy and grace, and our steadfast love and support.

A DIY life, without Christ, is lonely, difficult, unforgiving, and hopeless.

Facing the truth is difficult, but we cannot by our own power or might live a life of hope, love, forgiveness, or an abundant life. We need Jesus.

When we live in the word and promises of God, all things are possible.

Live in Christ, live in an abundant life where His love, hope, and everlasting life abound.

Thanks be to God.

Amen.

TRUSTING IN GOD

Trusting in God is difficult. Sometimes it feels like God is there for others, but not for me. I am a sinner and not worthy of His love. I am unlovable. When these thoughts come, Satan is at work trying his best to pull me away from God. He puts all the doubts and excuses in my thoughts and in my mind.

God says He loves me. He loves me so much He sent His only Son to die on the cross so I can live with Him forever. God says I am a forgiven sinner. He washes away all my sins and tells me I am worthy because He has already paid the price. He says He loves me even before He knew me. God loves me! God loves you! His word is true.

> And now, O Lord God, thou art God, and they words are true, and thou hast promised this good thing to thy servant. (2 Samuel 7:28)

> This God—His way is perfect, the promise of the Lord proves true; he is the shield for all those who take refuge in Him. (Psalm 18:30)

> But the anointing which you received from Him abides in you, and you have no need that any one should teach you; as His anointing teaches you about everything, and is true, and it is no lie, just as it has taught you, abide in Him. (1 John 2:27)

God loves each of us. He is our Savior and Lord who forgives our sins through His boundless mercy and grace. We believe in Him through faith with the help of the Holy Spirit, who dwells with in us. When our focus is on God and His word, we grow in trust, faith, and knowledge. We learn to believe, trust, live, and pray to our Lord and Savior, Jesus. We lose our way when we lose our focus and start to trust in meaningless harmful pleasures of the world or trust in those who try to pull us away from Jesus. Following Jesus and trusting is His love, forgiveness, and mercy is a far better way. God is trustworthy, steadfast, true, and He will never fail us.

He listens to His people, answers them, and supplies them with all their needs.

God shows us His love and trustworthiness over and over again by His grace, faithfulness, forgiveness, and goodness. He provides for us, He promises to always be with us, and He teaches us everything that is true.

God is always with us and helps us as we grow in faith. Live in His love and trust in His word and promises. He is the Way, which is more perfect, trustworthy and true. Trust in God.

Thanks be to God

Amen.

CHALLENGES

The world is a difficult place to live in. Every day we all face problems and challenges that can be small or large and someway seem unsolvable. Daily challenges include work, coworkers, finances, children, relationships, disease, homelessness, or aging. Other challenges include discipline to read the Bible, pray, and have devotions daily. Forgiving and being kind to others is also challenging. Challenges come in all sizes, shapes, and forms. Challenges can weigh heavy on our heart, mind, and soul. They even affect our attitude and behavior. We tend to *totally* focus on our own problems and challenges.

> For thou hast been my help, and in the shadow
> of thy wings I sing for joy. My soul clings to thee,
> thy right hand up holds me. (Psalm 63:7–8)

> Cast your anxieties on him, for he cares for you.
> (1 Peter 5:7)

Instead of focusing on the challenge, focus on Christ, Seek Him, watch for His help, and obey Him. Remember, God is faithful and His word is trustworthy.

Remember His help from the past, and in so doing, you know He reassures and strengthens us to face our current challenges. With Christ, challenges become manageable and solvable. Plans can even change, then a new dreams arises, and a new direction and path is found. We still must grieve the loss of old plans and dreams, but then we need to move forward with God, trusting Him to guide and direct us to a better path.

We keep our eyes on Christ Jesus, focus on Him, and trust in Him, His promises, His Word, and in His love for each of us. We face challenges daily, but with Christ, and without a doubt, He keeps His word as our deliverer, our rescuer, our refuge, our answer, our strength, and our wisdom.

Jesus promises to be with us and help us through all our challenges.

Thanks be to God.

Amen.

DECEIVING OURSELVES

We lie to ourselves. We deceive ourselves in believing untruths. We say we are unworthy; therefore, we can never lose weight or find a significant other. We continually fear and worry about everything and then tell ourselves that that is how God must want us to live. We lie to ourselves. We deceive ourselves into thinking we can get away with this or that if no one sees. We lie to ourselves. We become our own worst enemy.

Martin Luther states, "Lying is like a snowball, the longer you roll in it, the larger it becomes."

> Do not lie to one another seeing that you have put off the old nature with its practices. (Colossians 3:9)

> Whoever knows what is right and fails to do it, for him it is sin. (James 4:17)

> For the time is coming when people will not endure sound teaching, but have itching ears, they will accumulate for themselves teachers to suit their own likings. (2 Timothy 4:3)

> If we say we have fellowship with Him while we walk in darkness, we lie and do not live according to the truth. (1 John 1:6)

God abides in us, and when we abide in Him, He is our Father, our Lord and Savior, our confidant and friend. God is truth and never lies or deceives. God is faithful and just, and in Him, there is no sin. We can talk to Him. He knows our struggles. And when we let Him into our heart and mind, He provides us with His love, peace, courage, strength, and a spirit of truth to know right from wrong.

God's steadfast love for us is forever, and we can trust Him to help us and provide for our every need.

Live in God's forgiveness rather than our own deceitfulness.

Live in God's love, mercy, grace, and truth rather than in our own lies and feelings.

Live in God's words and promises rather than in our own insights.

Live in God-given faith rather than in our own doubts.

Live in and be confident in God's love, who was, is, and is to come rather than in our own insecurities. God does not deceive.

Live in the true, forgiving, and saving love and grace of Jesus Christ, our Savior and Lord.

Thanks be to God.

Amen.

POWER ON OUR KNEES

I hear some people still get down on their hands and knees to scrub floors. They claim the floors get cleaner. Other people get down on one knee to talk to small children.

When down on a knee, one is eye level with a small child, and it is easier to connect and relate to that child. Other people get down on their knees to weed their garden because they can get more of the root and, therefore, get rid of more weeds.

We go down to our knees when things get overwhelming or when everyday stress gets too much. We go down to our knees without a sound or with just barely an audible sigh. On our knees, we call on God for help. On our knees we surrender our control over our life to God. When we pray on our knees, He hears our inner voice seeking and asking for help without saying a word. God hears and answers our pleas and sighs. He gives strength and endurance to the tired and weak.

He gives comfort to the suffering mind, body, and soul. He gives peace to the troubled spirit. He gives love to all, especially the lost and lonely. He helps us through all our circumstances. He calms our fears, frees and strengthens us to endure and to continue to move through and forward all things.

There is power on our knees in prayer before God.

> Out of my distress I call on the Lord, the Lord
> answered me and set me free. (Psalm 118:5)

For this reason I bow my knees before the Father from whom every family in heaven and on earth is named, according to the rules of His glory He may grant you to be strengthened with might through His Spirit in he inner man. (Ephesians 3:14–15)

O come let us worship and bow down, let us kneel before the Lord our Maker. (Psalm 95:6)

There is power on our knees in prayer before God.

We kneel before God to worship, praise, and honor Him from a heart that is overwhelmed with gratitude, thanks, and love. We bow down in humility and adoration thanking Him for helping us and giving us life, strength, and courage.

There is power on our knees in prayer before God.

Thanks be to God.

Amen.

WISDOM

To the only wise God be glory for evermore through Jesus Christ. (Romans 16:17)

But the wisdom from above is first pure, then peaceable, gentle, open to reason, full of mercy, and good fruits, without uncertainty or insincerity. (James 3:17)

If any of you lack lacks wisdom, let him ask God who gives to all men generously and without reproaching, lacking in nothing. (James 1:5)

Trust in the Lord with all your heart, and do not rely on your own insight. In all your ways acknowledge Him, and He will make straight you paths. (Proverbs 3:5–6)

I take pride in my knowledge and wisdom. I usually want to one-up the next person so they know that I know more than them. And at that point, God is put on the back burner and *I* take over. I end up trying to glorify myself rather than God.

In the Bible, wisdom comes from God. God is the only one who grants true wisdom and knowledge. Our own wisdom cannot even come close to the wisdom of God because it is limited. We always seek and want more knowledge and wisdom. Our human wisdom does not compare to the all-knowing wisdom of God. We will never find what we are seeking without God. God's wisdom is pure, true, and sound. He gives us a wisdom from on high and a sense of what is right and wrong. As a human being, we can be wrong in our knowledge and wisdom, but God is never wrong. He guides and directs us to a path that helps us achieve our goal or to solve our situation or problem. The path in which He leads us is to a life that includes love, forgiveness, and peace in Him. He is never wrong, for which we glorify God.

When we walk daily with God and seek Him, we learn through our experiences that God provides unlimited stability, peace, and wisdom when we ask in His name.

Do not be wise in our own understanding, but allow God to share His wisdom with us. The wisdom of the Gospel fills our heart and mind.

Be wise and let God guide and direct our steps and way to a better path.

Let God be our wisdom and our truth.

Thanks be to God.

Amen.

THOUGHTS

Repay no one evil for evil, but take thought for what is noble in the sight of all. (Romans 12:17)

My thoughts are not your thoughts, neither are your ways my ways, says the Lord. (Isaiah 55:8)

Finally, brethren whatever is true, whatever is honorable, whatever is just, whatever is pure, whatever is lovely, whatever is gracious, if there is any excellence, if there is anything worthy of praise, think about these things. (Philippians 4:8)

What posts do you put online or on your tablet or your phone? What pictures do you post? What words do you post? Our posts can be an extension of our thoughts, our thinking, and what we are about. Posts can be positive or negative, and we put it all out there for anyone and everyone to see. It is a reflection of what we think is important. Sometimes it gives others the wrong idea and can lead them astray. Those negative thoughts and ideas can also turn us away or take us away from Christ and His love.

With help from God, we need to take control of what we print, say, and think. We need to fill our minds, heart, and thoughts with the love of God, His word and His life-giving truth. When we focus on Christ, our thoughts, actions, and deeds are of Christ.

Focus on Christ and the things of Christ, which are pure, noble, true, and uplifting and encouraging to all.

Thanks be to God.

Amen.

STEP ASIDE

Trust in the Lord with all your heart, and do not rely on you own insight. In all your ways acknowledge him, and he will make straight you paths. (Proverbs 3:5–6)

The God who girded me with strength, and made my way safe. (Psalm 18:32)

But He said to me, "My grace is sufficient for you for my power is made perfect in weakness." I will gladly boast of my weakness, that the power of Christ may rest upon me. (2 Corinthians 12:9)

Our lives tend to get difficult. In all our wisdom, we think we can control and manage any situation that comes our way. However, many times we do not know all the circumstances of the whole situation. Many times situations arise in which we have no control, and life becomes overwhelming. And soon we acknowledge that our understanding and knowledge are limited. We need to call on God, learn to step aside, and let Him into our lives and our struggles. He loves us and is there to help us. We need to learn to trust and rely on Him and His infinite wisdom and understanding to handle and work out the situation and struggles, for He is able.

> Cast all your anxieties on Him, for he cares about
> you. (1 Peter 5:7)

God is faithful and just. He loves us and is always with us and will help us through all our struggles and difficulties. Step aside and let go of trying to help God. Let go of taking back the control of the situation. Step aside, trust, and allow God to handle the *whole* situation, in His way and in His time. Continue to believe, trust, pray, and rely on Him to guide and direct the path that is set before us. Step aside and let God be God. He is able to do far more than we could ask or think. Step aside and allow God, who loves us, to take care of us.

Our God, who was in the beginning, promises to guard and guide our coming and going from this time on and forevermore.

Thanks be to God.

Amen.

DESIRES, CRAVING, AND LONGINGS

Whom have I in heaven but thee? And there is nothing upon earth that I desire besides thee. (Psalm 73:25)

Oh God, thou art my God. I seek thee, my soul thirsts for thee; my flesh faints for thee, as a dry and weary land where no water is. (Psalm 63:1)

Jesus said to them, "I am the bread of life; He who comes to me will never hunger and he who believes in me will never thirst." (John 6:35)

Everyone craves one thing or another in their life. We may crave justice or fairness; some people crave attention or approval, some desire love, and others crave sugar or chocolate. Sometimes the craving is so intense, we lose all reason and logic and do whatever it takes to fulfill that craving or longing. Often those desires, longings, or hungers still exist, even after we think we fill them.

Jesus is the one and only one to truly satisfy our longings, desires, hunger, and cravings. He not only supplies all our everyday needs, but He also satisfies and supplies us with His love, peace, and joy. He fills our soul and heart with His word, truth, and promises.

He shows us the way to life with Him. It is a place where our heart and soul is at peace no matter what happens.

Jesus fills all our desires and cravings. Jesus provides us with the bread of life and living water for our craving spirit. With Jesus, we will never hunger or thirst.

When we diligently seek and allow Jesus to satisfy the cravings, the hunger, and thirst in our heart and soul, He answers. The love of Jesus—His goodness, peace, and the comfort that He offers and supplies—fills those longings and desires. Jesus is the one and only to provide rest for our weary soul and relief of our everyday burdens and cravings.

Thanks be to God. Amen.

ABIDE IN CHRIST

Abide in me, and I in you. As the branch cannot bear fruit by itself, unless it abides in the vine, neither can you, unless you abide in me. I am the vine, you are the branches. He who abides in me, and I in Him, he it is that bears much fruit, for apart from me you can do nothing. (John 15:4–5)

So we know and believe the love of God has for us. God is love, and he who abides in love abides in God, and God abides in him. (1 John 4:16)

You have been born anew, not of perishable seed but of imperishable, the living and abiding word of God. (1 Peter 1:23)

Abide is a word that carries with it a deep and powerful message in the Bible. To abide means that there is a dependency, a fellowship, and a relationship with Jesus.

God tells us in the scripture that abiding is like a vine and its branches. A branch is nothing apart from the vine. Branches abide *in* the vine and bears fruit. Those in or abiding in Christ receive blessings and grow and flourish in Christian life. Jesus, the vine, is our source and supplier of life. We, His children, the branches, abide in the vine to live and flourish and bear fruit.

The living word of God abides in us and moves through us to help us grow in love and put away our selfish desires. God provides us with love, grace, strength, and a willing spirit to love and serve others, like Jesus. He is able to open our heart, mind, and soul to love, to serve, and to be a blessing to others.

All things are possible when Christ abides in us and we in Him. Jesus, the vine, is the sustainer and source of life and love for us, His people, the branches.

Apart from Christ, we can do nothing.

Abide in Christ to have life and have it abundantly and to be a blessing to others.

Thanks be to God.

Amen.

NEVER ALONE OR
ON OUR OWN

No man shall be able to stand before you all the days of your life, as I was with Moses, so I will be with you; I will not fail or forsake you. (Joshua 1:5)

Have I not commanded you? Be strong and of good courage; be not frightened, neither be dismayed; for the Lord your God is with you wherever you go. (Joshua 1:9)

Fear not for I am with you, be not dismayed, for I am your God; I will strengthen you, I will help you, I will uphold you with my victorious right hand. (Isaiah 41:10)

We try to control and influence the stressful situation.

We try to manipulate the circumstances to benefit ourselves.

We try to manage everything in our life on our own.

We can't control or manage everything—no one can. God did not create us to handle everything on our own. As children of God, we turn our worries, concerns, and stresses over to Jesus. He promises to be with us and help us through all circumstances of life.

God loves and cares for each of us. He sustains us, and He is our strength and our endurance for every situation. He is able to handle and carry our every burden that worries us or attacks us. He gives us peace and comfort and is able to work all things together for good for those who love Him.

With God, we do not need to worry or need to be in control of every situation. He will and is able to handle all things. But our pride and selfishness creep back into our life, and soon we take back control of everything again. Things soon start to fall apart, and our stress and worry return. We realize that God is the only one that can truly help us. He is the only one that can relieve the stress and worry. Trust in Him and His love and faithfulness, and allow Him to work things out. He knows what is best for us. We need to do our part as we continue to pray and leave the rest to God.

Give it all to God, for He loves and cares for us. He helps replace fear, worry, and control with His truth, His word, and His promises. God is always with us, willing and waiting to help us when we seek and call on Him. God will never leave us alone or on our own.

Thanks be to God.

Amen.

CHRIST THE CENTER
OF OUR LIFE

God loves us and therefore is always with us. He holds our hand and stands beside us, guarding and protecting us all through our everyday life. And when God is with us, we become able to stand in the face of trials and insults and through everyday circumstances and struggles.

And we become able to show love, kindness, and gentleness to all, especially to those who are difficult.

When we live in Christ, we give hope to someone who has lost hope, give hugs to someone who has lost a loved one, give food and water to someone who has none, and we visit those in the hospital and provide comfort and support to them.

God is with us, and He is our help, our strength, and our support. As we keep Christ as the center of our life, trust in Him, rely on Him, and live in Him, He helps us grow in faith, live in Him, and become more Christlike in our actions and deeds. When we walk with God, His light and love shines through us for all to see and know of God's love.

Live in and for Christ.

Lord, thank You for Your love. Help each of us seek and find Your unending and boundless love and saving grace. Help us live a life that glorifies and honors You. Help us to let Your light shine through us. Help us to live in kindness, gentleness, truth, in God's word and promises. Help us to show others the love of Christ by our actions, deeds, and voice.

Thanks be to God.

Amen.

SECTION 5

*Growing in Faith
and in Christ*

GROW, DEVELOP, AND SHINE IN CHRIST

When we say yes to God, we say yes to believing and trusting in Him. At that point, our life begins to change. We draw nearer to Him, and He assures us of His love and salvation. He guides and directs us on a path in which we grow and mature in faith and shine to be a blessing to all. He informs and enlightens us about our Almighty God, our Heavenly Father, who loves us so much, He wants a personal relationship with each one of us. He opens our heart and mind to Him. He wants us to know and trust in Him.

He wants us to know He is always with us—to help, comfort, and strengthen us as we go through life.

When we choose to live in Christ and for Him, He blesses us with gifts. The gifts of God vary from person to person depending on His gracious mercy and love. We decide whether to use the gifts given or not. We choose whether or not to grow, prosper, and to shine in Christ and through our faith.

It is not easy walking in the way of Jesus. The road is narrow and difficult, but Jesus is always with us and helping us. But we still make questionable choices. We seek and try other things looking for answers, or we try one relationship or another, or we go from one addiction to another looking for answers to fill our holes and emptiness.

But we soon discover and recognize that Jesus is the answer. Jesus gives and supplies all our needs. He is the way, the truth, and light in this world of darkness. He lights the way to a path of love, peace, and joy even in the midst of our struggles. When we cling to Jesus, walk with Him, and trust and obey Him, we find our purpose, our worth, our identity, our joy, our strength, our endurance, and love.

May these meditations, talks, prayers and insights be a blessing to you.

A Song

A song has been stuck in my mind all week. It is a song by Josh Wilson called "I Refuse."

The chorus goes like this: "I can't sit around and wait for someone else to do what God has called me to do myself. Oh, I could choose not to move, but I refuse. I refuse."

> But the Lord said to me, do not say I am only a youth; for all to whom I send you, you shall go, and whatever I command you, you shall speak. Be not afraid of them, for I am with you to deliver you, says the Lord. (Jeremiah 1:7–8)

Jeremiah is chosen by God to be a prophet to all nations. Jeremiah's response to God is "I can't, for I am not a good speaker, and besides, I am too young." The Lord tells Jeremiah not to say "I can't" and "When I tell you to go and speak to someone, then go, and I the Lord will be with you and tell you what to say."

Jesus calls us just like Jeremiah, and He gives us what we need when we need it for our journey. But we often make or use many excuses not to go or take action.

There is plenty to do in God's kingdom. We need everyone, bringing their gifts and their willingness to do His work. We do not need to worry or be anxious because God reaches out and touches our lives and gives us the ability to do what He calls us to do.

God is calling. Go in his name.

We can stand by, close our eyes, and pretend everything is okay, or we can jump in and get to work and be God's hands and feet. By stepping out in faith, we serve God and trust in Him to supply all our needs.

Listen, trust, obey, move, and act in his name.

Thanks be to God.

Amen.

ACTION WHILE WAITING

I waited patiently for the Lord; he inclined to me and heard my cry. He drew me up from the desolate pit, out of the miry bog, and set my feet upon a rock, making my steps secure. He put a new song in my mouth, a song of praise to our God. Many will see and fear, and put their trust in the Lord. (Psalm 40:1–4)

Watch and pray that you may not enter temptation; the spirit indeed is willing, but the flesh is weak. (Matthew 26:41)

We hear about people waiting for a new job, for a new opportunity, for a conflict to end, to buy a house, or to get into a specific school. Waiting for something to happen is part of everyday life.

While we wait, we pace, we fret, groan and moan, and even complain about waiting. While we wait, we tire, we give up, become idle, or complacent.

But at other times, we take action and get going and do the work, whatever it may be.

We practice or study and persevere to reach the final goal. It is our choice as to whether we sit, complain, and do nothing or we get up and get going.

We call upon the Lord to help us, but we want Him to answer immediately, and we want Him to solve our problem for us. God doesn't work that way. He will help us and supply our needs, but we need to do our part. When we call on the Lord, we need to wait for Him to work in His time and place. We are in this together, so whatever we do, first we pray. We pray constantly, take action, and let God open and close doors for us. Action and prayer work together so God can work in and through us.

We act by stepping forward in obedience, trusting in God and His promises. We step away from idleness and complacency. We pray, talk to God, worship, serve, and listen to Him. He will be with us to help us and to take care of us because that is His promise to His children. As we persevere in our actions and move forward in faith, we become more aware of God speaking to us in the still small voice of the Holy Spirit. It is the voice of truth, giving us guidance and direction for our lives.

As we wait on the Lord, pray and trust in Him for all good things.

Thanks be to God.

Amen.

EXPECTATIONS

He has showed you, O man, what is good; and what does the Lord require of you but to do justice, and to love kindness, and to walk humbly with God? (Micah 6:8)

And God is able to provide you with every blessing in abundance, so that you may always have enough of everything and may provide in abundance for every good work. (2 Corinthians 9:8)

As it is my eager expectation and hope that I shall not be at all ashamed, but that with full courage now as always Christ will be honored in my body, whether by life or by death. (Philippians 1:20)

What is it that you expect? From yourself? From others? From God?

We expect God to do many things in our life. But do we believe, trust, and expect Him to perform miracles and do the extraordinary things in our life and in the world?

God is God. He is powerful, faithful, mighty, and He fulfills His words and promises. He is our Savior and Lord and Almighty God. He is the one who gives us new life and transforms our heart and selfish behaviors. He changes those who don't want to and those who think that they can't change. He is able to love, forgive, guide, and direct us on a path that only He is able to give. Truly our God is able to do more than we can ever imagine.

Just as we expect things from God, He expects us, His children, to love, believe, trust, and obey Him. He expects us to love our neighbors and be a blessing to others. He wants us to give generously to those in need and to spread His word. He calls us to be His hands, His feet, His voice, and His presence in a world in darkness.

Our expectations of God is sometimes too small, and we forget His promises to always be with us to help us through all situations. We need to expect daily help from God, expect miracles from Him, and expect the extraordinary from Him, for He is able. As we surrender to God, we need to seek more, ask more, hope more, and trust more in God. He is able to do and help more than we can ever imagine.

Accept God at His word and expect Him to do the impossible and the extraordinary in each of our lives. Expect God to work in our lives, for He is able to do far more than we can ask or think.

Thanks be to God.

Amen.

POWER OF GOD THROUGH US

> But they who wait for the Lord shall renew their strength, they shall mount up with wings like eagles, they shall run and not be weary, and they shall walk and not faint. (Isaiah 40:31)

> Do not be conformed to this world but be transformed by the renewal of your mind that you may prove what is the will of God, what is good and acceptable and perfect. (Romans 12:2)

Showing others the way of truth and life is a path that God gives to us, His children. Our path is difficult, and the way is narrow and long. We may get lost from time to time, but when we constantly seek God, read His Word, and pray for guidance, He helps us to stay on the right path. The journey is rough, treacherous, and difficult. We need Jesus's help to guide and direct us, give us rest, give us life-saving water to renew our spirit, and give strength and endurance for the journey.

A God of mercy, love, power, and forgiveness is always with us. He renews, restores, sustains, and protects us for our journey to be His hands and feet in this world.

With Christ and by His power, we forgive and serve others, help our neighbors, visit the sick, and give to the poor. We serve as

God guides and directs us. We step out in faith to serve others in the community and share the Good News of the love of God.

By the power and love of God in and through us, we share the love of Jesus and show others the light and way to Christ and His abundant love.

Thanks be to God.

Amen.

FLASHLIGHTS

Everyone loves to play with flashlights in the dark. They make shadows on the wall, make it possible to read books under blankets, or they become lights in a fort made out of blankets and chairs. We use them with the grandkids while we sing songs. We use it specifically with the song "This Little Light of Mine." The chorus of the song goes, "Let it shine, let it shine, let it shine."

We swing our arms all over while holding the flashlight. The light moves all over the room. The light moves in circles, up and down, to the right and to the left. In some areas the light can barely be seen, and in other places, the darkest corners, it shines brightly.

> I am the Light of the world, he who follows me will not walk in darkness but will have the light of life. (John 8:12)

> Let your light so shine before, men, that they may see your good works and give glory to your Father who is in heaven. (Matthew 5:16)

> God is at work in you, both to will and to work for his good. Do all things without grumbling or questioning, that you may be blameless and innocent, children of God without blemish in the midst of a crooked and perverse generation,

among whom you shine as lights in the world.
(Philippians 2:13–15)

God's light shines through us, and we become "the light of the world." As children of God, others see, hear, and watch what we say and do. They don't always pay attention to what we say, but they do watch and pay attention to our actions and our works.

Our actions and good works hopefully coincide with what we say. Our actions and deeds hopefully glorify our Lord and Savior, not ourselves.

God is at work in us as He calls us to be His light in a world of darkness. Let God's light shine through each of us to a world in need.

Thanks be to God.

Amen.

LIVING IN GOD'S LOVE

> Be imitators of God, as beloved children, and
> walk in Love, as Christ loved us and gave himself
> for us, a fragrant offering and a sacrifice to God.
> (Ephesians 5:2)

Remember this line of the song, "Jesus loves me, this I know, for the Bible tells me so." All through the Bible, we hear of God's love for His children no matter what. He loves Moses even though he disobeyed Him. Daniel is mistreated and thrown into a lion's den for believing and trusting in God. David was a great ruler but sinned against man and God. God still loved them through everything; He forgave them when they repented.

God calls us to love others. But many times we attach conditions on our love because we are not perfect or because of our insecurities, flaws, or sinfulness.

It becomes "I will love you if…" "I love you, but…" This is not God's love.

God's love is unconditional. God's love is not dependent on what we are or what we do. God's love is a gift; it is perfect, pure, boundless, endless, patient, kind, and not jealous. God's love is boundless and everlasting.

God's wondrous love is for all.

When we become lost and overwhelmed by worldly things, seek God and His love.

When we cry out from our inner depths, He surrounds us with His love. He meets us where we are and provides for us. God's love is steadfast, unending, and unchanging. And when we abide in God's love and allow Him to renew and restore our body, heart, and mind, we become His light. A light for others to see His love and find the way to Him.

God loves us and abides in us. His love is everlasting. He calls us to love others, with a love that is patient, kind, and gentle, as He loves us.

Live in God's love.

Thanks be to God.

Amen.

LIVING IN GOD'S FORGIVENESS

It is so difficult to forgive. To forgive a sibling, a spouse, a child, or even a parent, a neighbor, or to forgive someone who has done you an injustice is almost impossible.

If we apologize, we must be wrong, or the other person thinks it. That kind of thinking is wrong, and Satan uses it against us. Satan does not want us to apologize, because without an apology, the situation ends badly, and everyone ends up hurt. The relationship suffers, and the longer there is no forgiveness or apology, the more broken the relationship becomes, and soon it becomes irreparable.

It says in 1 John 1:9, "If we confess our sins he is faithful and just to forgive our sins and cleanse us from all our unrighteousness."

When we ask for forgiveness, as it says in Psalm 103:13, "As far as the east is from the west, so far as He has removed our sins from us." This is the amazing love of God. Living in peace and in the forgiving love of Christ.

> Let all bitterness and wrath and anger and clamor and slander be put away from you, with all malice, and be kind to one another, as God in Christ forgave you. (Ephesians 4:31–32)

Be Christlike, as Colossians 3:12–17 says—put on compassion, kindness, lowliness, meekness, patience, forgiving each other, because the Lord has forgiven us.

As a child of God, He gives us the gift of forgiveness because we are a sinful people in need of forgiveness. We need God's mercy, love, and forgiveness, or we spend an eternity suffering from the consequences of our sinful self. Jesus takes the punishment we deserve by dying on the cross, and He saves us through His love, death, and resurrection. He redeems us and forgives when we ask in His name. But without God's mercy, grace, and forgiveness, our sin comes between God and us, and the relationship becomes broken. So when we accept and live in Christ, He forgives us and sets us free from condemnation and death, and we become a new creation in Him. Christ's love and His gift of forgiveness sets us free to love, forgive, and serve others.

The love and forgiveness of the Lord is forever and ever.

Live in peace and in God's forgiveness and in God's love. Share the amazing love and forgiveness of God with others.

Thanks be to God.

Amen.

WORTHY OF PRAISE

Our life is God's gift to us. God loves us so much, He gives and bestows on us, His children, grace upon grace, mercy upon mercy, and blessings on blessings. God's gifts and blessings overflow when we accept Jesus as our Lord and Savior. God's gift of faith is a life-changing event. When we believe and trust in Jesus, He liberates us from sin and sets us free from condemnation and slavery to sin. Thanks and praise to God.

> I therefore, a prisoner for the Lord, beg you to lead a life worthy of the calling to which you have been called, with all lowliness and meekness, with patience, forbearing on another in love. (Ephesians 4:1–2)

> Be watchful, stand firm in your faith, be courageous, be strong. Let all you that you do be done in love. (1 Corinthians 16:13–14)

> Finally, brethren, whatever is true, whatever is honorable, whatever is just, whatever is pure, whatever is lovely, whatever is gracious, if there is any excellence, if there is anything worthy of praise, think about these things. What you have learned and received and heard and seen in

me, do; and the God of peace will be with you.
(Philippians 4:8–9)

God's gift of love is boundless and everlasting. God's gift of strength is steadfast and enduring. Jesus continually forgives, renews, and refines us as forgiven children of God, through His love, forgiveness, mercy, and grace.

This is all ours and more because of Jesus Christ and as a child of God.

Our life is not always rosy, easy, wonderful, and happy. But through all of our ups and downs, God's promise is to be with us and supply all our needs in our daily walk with Him.

God's love for us is incomprehensible. His gifts, promises, words, mercy, grace, forgiveness, truth, strength, and peace is worthy of our praise.

Praise and glory to God, who loves, forgives, and blesses us.

Thanks be to God.

Amen.

FOCUS

Bless the Lord, O my soul, and forget not all
his benefits, who forgives all your iniquity, who
heals all your diseases, who redeems you life from
the Pit, who crowns you with steadfast love and
mercy, who satisfies you with good as long as you
live so that your youth is renewed like the eagle's.
(Psalm 103:2–5)

Looking to Jesus the pioneer and perfecter of
our faith, who for the joy that was set before him
endured the cross, despising the shame, and is
seated at the right hand of the throne of God.
(Hebrews 12:2)

At work, we were once asked to decorate a school bulletin board. So
we put a dot in the center of the four-by-six-foot board and wrote the
word FOCUS over the dot. We ended up redoing the board.

But think about it: what or where is the focus in our life?

As a child of God, Jesus is our focus, the center of our life.

It is important to keep our hearts and minds on Jesus Christ
because many things fight for our love and attention. In this world,
Satan wants to pull us away from Christ and His word. We get so
busy doing activities or doing our own thing, we forget about Christ
and what He wants us to do. And then our life gets out of control

because we try to do everything on our own and make everything perfect. The perfect never happens, and we have forgotten about Christ and His love. So instead of enjoying imperfect family time, dinner with friends and family, and serving others, we end up getting hurt and upset because nothing is perfect or right. Nothing is so important in this world that we forget Jesus and His love. Jesus gives us strength, comfort, and peace and takes care of us through the tough time and wants us to be a blessing to others.

So take time to pray, abide in His word, trust, and obey Him, grow in faith, and focus on Christ. Focus on Him rather than ourselves, so when trials and struggles come, Christ is our comforter, strength, and help.

> Let us fix our eyes on Jesus, the author and perfecter of our faith. (Hebrews 12:2)

Focus on Jesus. He helps us keep our hearts and minds on him by loving us, always being with us, helping us, and forgiving us. He continually supplies and equips us with all we need for our journey together. Focus on Jesus as He helps us to grow in faith and in love to serve others.

Look to Jesus, focus on Him, the one who loves, forgives, helps, protects, and blesses us.

Thanks be to God.

Amen.

HARVESTING

He who is kind to the poor lends to the Lord, and He will repay him for his deeds. (Proverbs 19:17)

As for what was sown on good soil, this is he who hears the word and understands it; he indeed bears fruit and yields, in one case one hundred-fold, in another sixty, and in another thirty. (Matthew 13:23)

And let us not grow weary in well-doing, for in due season we shall reap, if we do not lose heart. (Galatians 6:9)

Harvesting is the end of the growing season. Harvesting fruits, vegetables, grains, and other items from the field, orchard, or garden. Once the harvesting is done, the work of preparing items for use in the future begins. It needs to be washed, cleaned, and prepared in a certain way so the product remains good and usable at a later date.

God chooses us, equips us with the Holy Spirit, and supplies us with all we need as we share in His ministry. God chooses us, prepares us, and sends us out where there is a need. He supplies, fills, and equips us with anything and everything we need. He provides us His word, forgiveness, mercy, love, power, strength, peace, kindness, goodness, gentleness, self-control, and the ability to talk to Him at any time and place so we can plant His love and be a blessing to others.

God calls us to spread His word and to show others by our actions and deeds, His love.

We visit the homebound, speak kindly, and share His word to our neighbors and enemies through our actions and deeds. The word is heard and understood, and then the "harvest" is by the power of the Holy Spirit.

He calls us, one and all, in His name to spread His word and to bear fruit for Him.

All to His Honor and Glory.

Thanks be to God.

Amen.

NEVER FLAG IN ZEAL

> Never flag in zeal, be aglow with the spirit, serve
> the Lord. (Romans 12:11)

Zeal means enthusiastic and a diligent pursuit of God and His will.

We need to be immediate and urgent in what we do. We do not give up when things get tough—just get on your knees and ask God to renew our zeal and fire for Him.

Modern furnaces take the work out of keeping warm in the cold. We simply set the thermostat, and the house is warm when we get up in the morning. In earlier days, they tended to the fire constantly and carefully and monitored the fuel because running out could be deadly.

The same is true spiritually. If we think our spiritual fire is ignited as easily as a modern furnace, we run the risk of running out of spiritual fire and zeal. We need to tend and nourish our spirit as well as our physical body.

To recapture our zeal, or our enthusiasm, we must start by focusing on Jesus. When our zeal tank is running low or empty, or we lose our enthusiasm for life, or we feel stuck or lost, we need to call on Jesus for help. We turn to Jesus and focus on Him when we lose our purpose, our joy, or lose sight of what He calls us to do.

We burn out easily because we do not constantly monitor our spiritual life. We take our eyes off Jesus; we let up and begin to coast. We do not finish what we start because we get distracted and other things take priority. We must remain faithful, loving and serving our Lord and Savior. We cannot take our spiritual life for granted, or it will grow cold when we fail to supply it with fuel.

We need to fan the fire within and keep the spirit fueled and aflame through prayer, God's word, praise, confession, and thanksgiving. Keep the fire ablaze to prevent our spirit from sinking.

Focus on God and our commitment to Him, then our zeal and our enthusiasm returns. We live passionately for Jesus and do the work He calls us to do.

When He calls and sends us to serve and spread God's love and mercy, we continue the ministry of Christ with zeal.

The renewal of spirit brings us new love, new hope, new peace, and a new vision for tomorrow.

Never flag in zeal, be aglow with the spirit, serve the Lord.
Thanks be to God.
Amen.

FACE OF JESUS

No one really knows or has seen the face of Jesus. We see pictures that depict Him as a man with blond hair, blue eyes, and a beard. Other pictures depict Him with dark hair, brown eyes, and a dark beard. In all the pictures, we see Him wearing a long robe and sandals.

The actual facial characteristics of Jesus is unknown to us. Maybe, just maybe, God wants it that way. Maybe God wants us to know Him by His love, actions, deeds, and works, rather than what He looks like.

He wants us to be the face of Jesus to others. Knowing what Jesus looks like may distract us from our responsibility to love others, do good works, be encouraging to one another.

> I am the good shepherd; 1 know my own and my
> own know me. (John 10:14)

> By this we know love, that He laid down His life
> for us; and we ought to lay down our lives for the
> brethren. (1 John 3:16)

Be the face of Jesus to others.

Be the face of Jesus by sharing the love of Jesus with someone and giving them hope when they feel all is lost.

Be the face of Jesus by hugging someone who has just lost a loved one.

Be the face of Jesus by smiling at someone who is not smiling or looks sad.

Be the face of Jesus by giving a coat to someone who has none.

The world needs Jesus. The world needs us to be the hands and feet of Jesus.

Let God's light shine through us today and every day.

Let God use us each and every day as an instrument of His love, peace, comfort, and strength.

Be the face of Jesus to all.

Thanks be to God.

Amen.

Grow Where You
Are Planted

There is a saying, "Grow where you are planted." You see it printed on pictures and painted on wood hangings. There is a picture from the Skagit Valley Tulip Festival that shows row after row of red tulips in bloom, and there in the bottom right-hand comer is one yellow tiny tulip in full bloom. It is all by itself, the only yellow tulip in a field of red. You might miss it, but it is there, when you look closely.

As Christians, sometimes we may feel like that tiny yellow tulip, all by itself. We try to deal with everything and everyone by ourselves. We think that maybe if we were there or over there, things would be different. Maybe it would be better or more fun in another place. We have forgotten about God and do not think about Him or His promises to us.

> Not that I complain of want, for I have learned,
> in whatever state I am, to be content. I know how
> to be abased, and I know how to abound; in any
> and all circumstances I have learned the secret of
> facing plenty and hunger, abundance and want.
> I can do all things in Him who strengthens me.
> (Philippians 4:11–13)

Keep your life free from the love of money, and
be content with what you have, for he has said,
"I will never fail or forsake you." (Hebrews 13:5)

When we turn and give our lives over to God, we live our lives honoring and serving Him. As we abide in and with God, He gives us strength and empowers us for our journey. So no matter where we are, God uses each of us for His glory, and we find joy, peace, and contentment even in a field of red tulips.

Rejoice, be glad, and bloom. God promises of blessings upon blessings to those who believe and obey Him. Then the wanting and wishing of being here or there is less important, and serving God becomes more important. God is with us, supplying our every need and giving us gifts beyond our wildest dream, to fulfill our desires and accomplish the tasks set before us wherever it may be.

For I know the plans I have for you, says the
Lord, plans for welfare and not for evil, to give
you a future and a hope. (Jeremiah 29:11)

Sometimes we are in a place that is strange or troubling or fearful. But as God's children, we are always in His hands. He is always with us, taking care of us and giving us strength and courage to live in His love, word, and promises.

Grow and bloom even in a field of red tulips.

Thanks be to God.

Amen.

LIGHTHOUSE

A lighthouse stands strong among waves and wind.

A lighthouse emits light to mark a dangerous coastline, a shoal, a reef, or it marks a safe entry into a harbor.

With God, we too stand strong in His strength and power, in His word, promises, and in faith, trust, and hope.

With God, we stand strong against false teachings and thinking, gossip, and bad habits.

With God, we stand strong against the wind and storms that daily assail us.

With God, we stand strong emitting God's light for others to see and follow.

With God, we stand strong against things that pull us away from God's love.

With God, we stand strong as we let God guide and direct our path to a life with Him that is rich, full, and everlasting.

Stand strong with God and as His light in this world.

> Be watchful, stand firm in your faith, be courageous be strong. Let all that you do be done in love. (1 Corinthians 16:13–14)

Thanks be to God.
Amen.

GRAVITY

Gravity by definition is a force that tries to move or pull objects toward each other. Gravity keeps us grounded so we do not float away. Gravity is what causes objects to fall. Sin also can weigh us down and cause us to pull away from God or fall. So the gravity of the situation is that we need God to take away our sin that weighs us down. We need His abundant love and forgiveness to wash away our sins.

> For by grace you have been saved through faith;
> and this is not your own doing, it is the gift of
> God. (Ephesians 2:8)

> If we confess our sins, he is faithful and just,
> and will forgive our sins and cleanse us from all
> unrighteousness. (1 John 1:9)

We need to ground ourselves in Jesus Christ and to live a life of faith in Him. Things of this life fall away, and people turn against us, but Jesus is steadfast and faithful. His love and promises never cease. He is our Savior and Lord.

Jesus takes away our sin, our resentments, our anger, our unhealthy dependencies, and our old baggage. We do not need to cheat, lie, be anxious, or be depressed or worry.

We ground ourselves in Christ, and His promises of grace and mercy is abundant and free. His promise of forgiveness gives us life, peace, comfort, strength, and joy—for all who believe and trust in Him.

We anchor ourselves in Christ, He abides in us, and we trust in Him to always be with us through all the ups and downs of life.

Our hope is in the Lord, who is and will always be with us.

> Let us hold fast the confession of our hope without wavering, for he who promised is faithful. (Hebrews 10:23)

Thanks be to God.
Amen.

NEW EVERY MORNING

There is a saying, "Every morning has a new beginning, a new blessing, a new hope, God's gift."

> The steadfast love of the Lord never ceases, his mercies never come to an end; they are new every morning; great is thy faithfulness. (Lamentations 3:22–23)

God's love and mercy is new every moment of every day. Every moment with God is new. God knows each one of us. He knows we fail, sin, and disobey. But when we confess our sins, He bestows on us love, mercy, grace, forgiveness, a new beginning, and a new life in Him. God fulfills His promises to His children.

First John 1:9 says that all we have to do is ask, and His forgiveness washes our sin away, and we are clean again by the power of the Holy Spirit.

Every moment is a new moment by the grace, mercy, and love of God.

Just as we struggle daily, the prophet Jeremiah struggles daily, according to the Old Testament. He tells people of different cities what God tells him to say to them. Not everyone likes what He has to say. So He is put into the stocks. And later, he is threatened with death. But through it all, Jeremiah continues to tell the people about God. Jeremiah realizes through it all that God is always with

Him, bringing new love, new mercy, new beginnings, and hope. All Jeremiah needs is God.

All we need is God; His mercy, love, grace, and forgiveness never runs out. God is faithful, and His love endures forever.

God cares for His children daily, moment by moment.

Just as Jeremiah learns to trust and rely on God, we too grow in faith and learn to rest our hope, our love, our peace, our salvation in God every day.

All we need is God, moment by moment.

God's love and mercy is for us, and it is new every morning.

Thanks be to God.

Amen.

Eye on the Ball

The coach at all the ball games yell, "Keep your eye on the ball."

In other words, "pay attention," "watch the ball all the time so you are ready to do your part during the game."

We want God to attend to us, but do we attend to God and what he wants us to be or do? Maybe we attend only at our own convenience or during a crisis.

> Having the eyes of your hearts enlightened, that you may know what is the hope to which he has called you, what are the riches of his glorious inheritance in the saints. (Ephesians 1:18)

> Be attentive to my words, incline you ear to my sayings. (Proverbs 4:20)

> I lift my eyes to the hills. From whence does my help come? My help comes for the Lord, who made the heaven and earth. (Psalm 121:1–2)

Jesus wants us to keep our eyes, our focus, on Him. He wants us to be attentive to Him at all times because things pull us away from Him. We can falter and lose sight of Him and our path when we lose focus. As we focus on Jesus, our trust and faith grows. Our actions, words, and deeds become reflections of God's love and light.

We keep our eyes on Jesus and follow Him as He guides and directs us with love on a path to abundant life and hope that is everlasting. When we listen to His word, we find forgiveness, mercy, grace, and hope.

We keep our eyes on Jesus; it is where we find our strength, courage, and help.

Thanks be to God.

Amen.

DAYLIGHT SAVINGS TIME

Daylight savings time refers to certain times of the year when we "fall back and spring forward."

In our life with Christ, we learn to "spring forward" or step out in faith. When we step out in faith, we trust and "fall back" on God, relying on His words and promises.

Be bold, take the first step, "spring forward" in faith. It is time to take a risk and see what happens when we open our heart to trust God. God can't act if we don't take a risk and step forward. If we don't take a step, nothing happens, because without risk, there is no reward. When we step out of our comfort zone and take the first step with God, He equips us for all things.

> What then shall we say to this? If God is for us, who is against us? (Romans 8:31)

> But you are a chosen race, a royal priesthood, a holy nation, God's own people, that you may declare the wonderful deeds of him who called you out of darkness into his marvelous light. (1 Peter 2:9)

God fills us when we are empty. He strengthens us when we are weak. His arms surround us with love to give us courage and comfort as we step out and forward in faith to do the work He calls us to do. Now is the time to spring forward in faith and fall back on God's love and strength and promises and do the work God calls us to do. Take the step forward, rely on God, and experience a closer walk with Him.

Thanks be to God.

Amen.

NORTHERN LIGHTS

The northern lights are sometimes known as the "dancing light." The dancing light is a collision of electrically charged particles from the sun that enters the earth's atmosphere. However, the Inuits of Alaska believe the lights come from the spirit of the animals they hunt. Others believe the lights come from the spirits of their people.

> But you are not in the flesh, you are in the spirit, if the spirit of God really dwells in you. Anyone who doesn't have the spirit of Christ does not belong to Him. But if Christ is in you—although your bodies are dead because of sin, your spirits are alive because of righteousness. (Romans 8:9–10)

> For all who are led by the spirit of God are Sons of God. (Romans 8:14)

> For God, who said, "Let light shine out of darkness," made His light shine in our hearts to give us the light of knowledge of the glory of God in the face of Jesus Christ. (2 Corinthians 4:6)

God enters the world and our lives and shakes up the status quo.

God collides with our culture and traditions and calls us to abide in Him, as He abides in us. God calls us to be a spirit of truth, righteousness, and His light in this world of darkness.

We grow and mature in faith when we abide in Him and He in us. When we walk with Jesus, we walk in the word, the spirit of faith, the spirit of the truth, and in the spirit of righteousness. When we walk with Jesus, the love and truth of God shines through us for others to see and know the love of God.

The spirit of God dwells in us and reflects the light of Jesus to others, to a world in darkness.

Thanks be to God.

Amen.

AHA MOMENTS WITH GOD

An aha moment is an epiphany. It is a moment when you understand or realize an insight about God, and it changes your life. Aha moments happen suddenly; out of nowhere, we realize God impacts our life and our walk with Him. God is always with us, abiding and working to reveal His love, knowledge, wisdom, and understanding to us that we were unaware of before or was beyond our reach.

Suddenly our eyes are open, and a new sight is seen, and we become able to see what we could not see before. Our life changes in that moment because of God and His love.

And we realize that the job we wanted so desperately and did not get was part of God's answer to our prayer. Another door opens, and a new opportunity arises. It brings a new and different dream, with a new direction, and with it, a new and better job. It also comes with better pay and benefits, an aha moment. Or we suddenly realize it is God who protects us while driving on the freeway, when an out-of-control car just misses you and your car. There is no other explanation, it is God, an aha moment. It is life changing and sends you toward God in thankful praise.

> The fear of the Lord is the beginning of wisdom,
> and the knowledge of the Holy one is insight.
> (Proverbs 9:10)

> Now when Jesus was born in Bethlehem of Judea
> in the days of Herod the king, behold, wise men
> from the East came to Jerusalem, saying, "Where
> is he who has been born king of he Jews? For we
> have seen a star in the East, and have come to
> worship him." (Matthew 2:1–2)

Just like the wise men in Matthew 2:1–2 in the Bible. The wise men, known as magi and astrologers of that time, did not believe in a Messiah. However, they heard about this Jesus, King of the Jews. They had an aha moment, and they followed the star to Bethlehem to worship Jesus. This becomes a life-changing epiphany for them. God reveals to them that truly this Jesus born is their Savior. God not only transforms the wise men, but also the Gentiles and nonbelievers, into people of God.

God brings life-changing, aha moments to all people to inspire, encourage, and transform their lives.

> For He has made known to us in all wisdom
> and insight the mystery of His will, according
> to His purpose which he sets forth in Christ.
> (Ephesians 1:9)

Thanks be to God.
Amen.

FISHING

Fishing is an American pastime. Many people enjoy fishing and communing with nature out on the water.

To fish, one needs to be prepared and have the right equipment. This includes a pole, line, sinker, hooks, bait, a net, and maybe a boat. One needs to know the type of fish one is fishing for, the bait they like, and the environment each type of fish likes. Then one needs to step out on the dock, shore, or boat and cast the line and wait patiently because fish do not always bite.

> And He said, "Follow me and I will make you
> fishers of men." (Matthew 4:19)

Jesus calls us to His service and to follow Him. When we follow Jesus, we become fishers of men. And just like fishing for fish, to be a fisher of people requires one to be prepared. To do God's will and work, first we need to know God, His love and purpose. We read and study the Bible to learn the message of Jesus, the cross, and His power to forgive sins and the good news of the Bible. We need to remember our own faith story and be willing to share it. However, being a fisher of people is difficult, so we must also protect ourselves by putting on the whole armor of God. Then we step out in faith and in word of God and to share His love to neighbors and the community even when they do not want to hear or listen.

When ministering to a world in need, we must also be willing to provide for the whole person, which includes their physical needs. Many times the physical needs of food, clothing, and shelter is more important and the only thing on their mind. Physical needs must be met first before someone is willing to hear about the love God. Meeting the physical needs of people is also another way to show God's love to them by using actions rather than words.

Follow God, trust and believe in His mission and message. Step off the dock and into the boat, and go out in the water and throw out the line and wait. Show others the love and mercy of God through kindness, goodness, and forgiveness, saving grace, and patience. Share your faith in words, actions, and deeds. Show others Jesus, the light of the world, and let the Holy Spirit and God do the rest.

Thanks be to God.

Amen.

GLISTEN, SPARKLE, SHINE

Let thy face shine on thy servant; save me in thy
steadfast love. (Psalm 31:16)

Let your light so shine before men, that they
may see your good works and give glory to your
Father who is in heaven. (Matthew 5:16)

That you may be blameless and innocent, children
of God without blemish in the midst of a crooked
and perverse generation, among whom you shine
as lights in the world. (Philippians 2:15)

The needles and leaves in the trees glisten, sparkle, and shine in the
sun after it snows or rains. It is bright, glorious, and beautiful.

As children of God, we too glisten, sparkle, and shine in the
light of Jesus. We reflect the love and light of Jesus for all to see
at any time. We choose by our actions, manners, attitude, smiles,
demeanor, deeds, and by our language who we want others to
see. We portray selflessness rather than selfishness with the help
of Jesus. We want others to see our good works and know Jesus is
in our life.

As we go through the day, glisten, sparkle, and shine with the
light of Jesus. Our expressions and actions reflect the light and
love of Jesus for all to see, and then they too will want to know

Jesus Christ as their Savior and Lord. Praise, honor, and glory to Jesus, who is our light.

Thanks be to God.

Amen.

Honor and Glory to God

Do we give to an organization?

 Do we give to the church?

 Do we build a new house?

 Do we buy a new car?

 Do we shovel the neighbor's walk?

 Do we visit the neighbor when He is sick?

 We always find something to do with our time, gifts, or our money. There is a variety of things to do with our time and money over our lifetime. There is always a choice, and making the right decision is difficult.

 How do we choose? Do we put all the choices in a hat and pull one or two out? Do we go with what the kids want? Do we research all the possibilities and pick the best one, or do we procrastinate on making a decision?

 Or we can take the decision to the Lord in prayer. We ask Him for help and guidance in making the decision. If we make a decision without God, it is in all likelihood selfish, and it tends to glorify ourselves. A decision we make with God, after prayer and deliberation, allows God to work in our lives, and it allows Him to open and close doors for us, to guide and direct our steps as we move forward in our decision. Our decisions made with God tend to be selfless and glorify God and His love for us.

> So, whether you eat or drink, or whatever you do, do all to the glory of God. (1 Corinthians 10:31)

> If we live by the Spirit, let us also walk by the Spirit. (Galatians 5:25)

> For from Him and through Him and to Him are all things. To Him be glory forever. Amen. (Romans 11:36)

> We who first hoped in Christ have been destined and appointed to live for the praise of His glory. (Ephesians 1:12)

When we accept Jesus as our Savior and Lord, everything we do—our work, our service, our job, our actions and deeds—is out of love for Him. We do not need to promote ourselves in any way but to show others and the world God's peace, respect, gentleness, kindness, love, and joy that God gives. We encourage and build one another up because of His love for us. We do all this to honor and glorify God for His steadfast love.

Thanks be to God.

Amen.

ARISE, GO

Arise, shine, for you light has come, and the glory of the Lord has risen upon you. (Isaiah 60:1)

Through Him we have obtained access to this grace in which we stand, and we rejoice in our hope of sharing the glory of God. (Romans 5:2)

And He said to him, "Rise and go your way; your faith has made you well." Arise and go. (Luke 17:19)

God calls each of to follow Him.

God calls us to arise and be doers in His kingdom.

God calls us to arise and go, trusting Him for all things.

He calls each of us according to our gifts and willingness to do His work.

It is time for each of us to get rid of our excuses and selfishness. Stop blaming others for not doing the work God calls us to do, and ask for His forgiveness.

It is time to listen to God and let Him work in your life. Get out of the safe environment. Arise and take a risk for Christ.

Arise, go and share the good news of Christ to all.

Arise, go and share your gifts for the good of all.

Arise, go and share your clothes and food to those in need.

Arise, go and seek the Lord for wisdom and knowledge.

Arise, go and share the love of Christ with others, just as He shows His love to you.

Arise, go and act out of a Spirit-led heart and mind to bless all you meet, for this is the only way others will know of the great love of God.

Arise, go and do all these things out of God's love and give Him honor and glory.

> Let your light so shine before men, that they may see your good works and give glory to your Father who is in Heaven. (Matthew 5:16)

Thanks be to God.
Amen.

GIVING OF OURSELVES

Give, and it will be given to you; good measure, pressed down, shaken together, running over, will be put in your lap. For the measure you give will be the measure you get back. (Luke 6:38)

And they sold their possessions and goods and distributed them to all, as they had need. (Acts 2:45)

Do not neglect to do good and to share what you have, for such sacrifices are pleasing to God. (Hebrew 13:6)

We do not have to go very far from home to see people in need. We see the homeless and people in need all over the city, in our schools, at work, at the stores, and in our neighborhoods.

We also see the opposite. Those who have plenty. Those who have what they need and buy what they want. They have a home, a car, a job, food, health. We see ourselves as part of those who have the things we need and even more. However, in an instant, we too can lose all things and become homeless and in need.

We give thanks to God for what He gives us. He gives us so much and does so much for us, there is always something for which we can give Him thanks. We thank God for family, our home, people in our life, food, friends, car, job, church, and health. The list is endless.

As God gives to us, He then charges us to help and give to others out of our love for Him and our bounty. God loves us all, so we then give of what we have to those in need. We show others through our actions and deeds Jesus's love.

> What you have learned and received and heard
> and seen in me, do; and the God of Peace will be
> with you. (Philippians 4:9)

Jesus is our example of ways to help others. His life is an example of ways to serve others and to show others of God's love. God calls us to do the same. We can volunteer at a shelter, give a ride to an elderly person to an appointment, mow someone's yard, help at a food gathering place, visit or call someone who has no one.

When we give of ourselves and of what we have and in any way we can, with humility and kindness, we help others and let God's love flow through us to them. And more important, we grow in faith and learn to be content and appreciate what God gives us.

Whether it is a lot or a little, give from the heart. God loves a cheerful giver. Giving from the heart not only makes a difference in someone else's life, but it makes a difference in our own life. Give generously from the heart.

Thanks be to God. Amen.

GIVE THANKS

Praise the Lord! O give thanks to the Lord for He is good, His steadfast love endures for ever! (Psalm 106:1)

Give thanks in all circumstances for this is the will of God in Christ Jesus for you. (1 Thessalonians 5:18)

You will be enriched in every way for great generosity, which through us will produce thanksgiving to God. (2 Corinthians 9:11)

In the Bible, Jesus heals ten lepers. He heals all of them, but only one comes back to give Him thanks. He is the only one that is grateful and thankful enough to give thanks to the healer, Jesus. The other nine leave without giving thanks. Their minds appear to be on other things. They do not seem to be grateful enough to give thanks.

Their hearts and mind are not on the love and blessing from Jesus.

Let us remember to always give thanks to God, the giver of all things. Let's remember to thank God for all the blessings He bestows on us, for all our daily needs, for the people in our lives, for His salvation, His forgiveness, His word, and His promises and His everlasting love.

According to Martin Luther, "The only thing we can give God is our thanks and gratitude."

Life is full of ups and downs, drama, tragedies, joys, sadness, sorrow, pain, and surprises. Through it all, our Lord and Savior is with us. No matter what, He never leaves us. He gives us strength, comfort, peace, and endurance as we go through life. So whether we live or whether we die, we are the Lord's. Nothing can separate us from the love of God. Give thanks to God and live triumphantly in Him.

Live, giving God thanks for His wondrous deeds for His children.

Live, giving God thanks for His love and for abundant life in Him—here, now, and always.

Thanks be to God.

Amen.

CHORES AND
RESPONSIBILITIES

Do all things without grumbling or questioning,
that you may be blameless and innocent, children of God without blemish in the midst of a
crooked and twisted generation, among whom
you shine as lights in the world. (Philippians
2:14–15)

Whatever your task, work heartily, as serving the
Lord, not men. (Colossians 3:23)

All things should be done decently and in order.
(1 Corinthians 14:40)

Within our family, everyone has chores to do from the youngest to
the oldest. No matter the size of the chore, big or small, or a chore
for one or more, everyone contributes, and we all get the chores done
together.

Children can be impulsive and selfish. They would rather play
than work or do chores. However, giving children chores, tasks, or a
chance to serve others gives them an opportunity to learn discipline,
obedience, and responsibility. They learn the value and satisfaction
of a job well done. Giving children chores or a chance to help gives
them a purpose and a sense of belonging to the family.

We too belong to God's family. Therefore, we too have chores and responsibilities. This may include ushering, cleaning, setting up, mowing, changing lightbulbs, or shoveling snow at the church, to name a few. As part of God's family, we also share in the responsibility in His ministry. This includes sharing with others the good news of Jesus as our Savior and Lord, being God's hands and feet in this world, and being a light in a world of darkness. This can take on many forms, but all the chores of sharing and serving gives us purpose and a sense of belonging to the family of God. We learn responsibility, discipline, and obedience. We learn to be hard workers and to be cheerful in all our serving.

We serve with a grateful and humble heart because of God's love.

We serve a Risen Savior who helps us in all our serving and ministry to be His light shining in this world.

Thanks be to God.

Amen.

CLING TO JESUS

My soul clings to thee; thy right hand upholds me. (Psalm 63:8)

Let love be genuine, hate what is evil, holdfast to what is good. (Romans 12:9)

Holding fast the word of life, so that in the day of Christ I am proud that I did not run in vain or labor in vain. (Philippians 2:16)

Moss grows all over in the Pacific Northwest. It is in, through, around, and over rocks, dirt, concrete, trees, or any other reasonably stable surface, as long as it has water for some part of the year. It is difficult to remove because of its threadlike cords that anchor it to a surface. Moss clings and anchors itself to many surfaces to live and survive.

We anchor ourselves to Jesus for safety, stability, love, and wholeness that He provides. We anchor and cling to Jesus, for He is our rock, our salvation, our Savior and Lord. Life in and with Jesus provides us with the way, the truth, and the light.

As we hold fast and cling to Jesus, He too holds on to us, His children. He is our rock and anchor. He supplies us with His love, grace, strength, mercy, forgiveness, His word and promises. We live in the love of Jesus, His hope and abundant life. No one can destroy our life with Jesus or take it away.

Cling to Jesus. Let Him uphold, uplift, strengthen you as you live a life unto Him.

Thanks be to God.

Amen.

CHARACTER

> More than that, we rejoice in our sufferings, knowing that suffering produces endurance, and endurance produces character, and character produces hope, and hope does not disappoint us, because God's love has been poured into our hearts through the Holy Spirit which has been given to us. (Romans 5:3–5)

Have you ever seen a piece of wood in a finished project that is amazing because of its beauty? The grain and the color of the wood is magnificent.

The character of the wood is in its color, luster, and grain. It is all determined by the growth pattern and rate of the growth of the tree. The more stress the tree endures due to drought, disease, fire, or proximity of other plants, the tighter the growth rings become and create more grain and character in wood products. The finish coat of oil on the wood brings out even more of the character of the wood.

We too have character. This is part of our makeup, our personality and identity given to us by God. But we become responsible for developing our character. Our character grows and is reflected by our attitude, our heart, and how we react to situations. We can lie down and quit when situations get difficult, or we can trust God and His help to guide and walk with us on the path toward a solution. Many times our stress and our difficulties push us toward God and

His help. We find ourselves trusting and relying on Him, rather than ourselves for a solution. He gives us strength to endure and persevere in all situations.

Stand fast with God, move forward, knowing God is with us, helping and supplying our every need. Our faith grows, and our heart, mind, and character become more Christlike. And through our faith, we reflect the heart and character of Jesus within us to others.

Thanks be to God.

Amen.

ENDURE

By your endurance you will gain your lives. (Luke 21:18)

More than that, we rejoice in our suffering, knowing that suffering produces endurance, endurance produces character, and character produces hope. (Romans 5:3–4)

As for you, always be steady, endure suffering, do the work of an evangelist, fulfill you ministry. (2 Timothy 2:10)

We always hear about hunting and fishing stories. Of course, everyone exaggerates the situation and outcome the more the story is told. The story is always about the size or the amount of the catch or about enduring the adventure with all its hardships. But through it all, no one gives up until they see or catch an animal or fish. It is about persevering and enduring everything for the catch. If one gives up and does nothing, the gain is nothing.

Part of Jesus's story is about enduring hardships for the sake of the Gospel. Jesus willingly endures the cross and grave for our salvation, regardless of the pain, because of His love for us. God helps us stand fast and endure trials and hardships. He helps us move forward and beyond the current situation or issues. As we endure hardships and struggles with God, we continually pray, cling to His word, promises, and truths. We trust in His power to work through us, through others, and through all circumstances to work everything out for us and to glorify Him for His boundless love.

As we endure circumstances and situations with God's help, we become God's light to others going through difficult times. We also become an encouraging light to those who become overwhelmed with their own struggles or to those who live in darkness.

Endure and persevere all things with God to gain life and hope and to be a blessing to others.

Thanks be to God.

Amen.

THANKS BE TO GOD

O give thanks to the Lord, for He is good; for His steadfast Love endures forever. (1 Chronicles 16:34)

Thanks be to God who in Christ always leads us in triumph, and through us spreads the fragrance of knowledge of Him everywhere. (2 Corinthians 2:14)

We thank our parents for gifts they give us. They give those gifts whether monetary or not, out of love. We purposefully thank them. We thank them out of our deep love and gratitude for them and the blessings they give us.

We too thank the Lord and give Him praise for all He does for us. The Lord gathers us in, saves us, forgives us, and blesses us. He is our source of love, strength, comfort, peace, and joy.

The Lord reigns. Let all rejoice. His mercy and love abound. Praise the Lord. Give thanks to the Lord for He is good. Let us all rejoice for the Lord cares and blesses His children. His salvation is for all who believe and trust in Him. His love is for all people and for all generations. Thanks be to God for His love and care for all. Thanks be to God, "for His steadfast love endures forever."

Thanks be to God.

Amen.

Flourish with Jesus

Be strong in the Lord and in the strength of His might. (Ephesians 6:10)

You received Christ Jesus the Lord, so live in Him, rooted and built up in Him and established in faith, just as you were taught, abounding in thanksgiving. (Colossians 2:6–7)

Lord is faithful, He will strengthen you and guard you from evil. (2 Thessalonians 3:3)

Learning to kayak or drive a car takes time and patience. It takes hours of practice to perfect and learn a new skill and the right equipment and a knowledgeable teacher to teach these skills to you. You need to learn, understand, and practice the rules of the road or water. You need to practice navigating in a variety of weather and water conditions with an experienced person. In time you too develop, mature, and flourish into the new skills.

Everyday life is difficult. Jesus is our help and guide as we navigate through our life journey. So we develop a relationship with Jesus. We follow Him and His word, talk and pray to Him, and give Him thanks for all He is and all He does for us. We believe and trust in Jesus as our friend, our supplier, sustainer, our supporter, and our Savior and Lord.

Jesus helps us to rely on Him as we face our everyday challenges. Our focus is on Him, and we stand boldly and steadfastly with Him. We face all our struggles and hardships together. Jesus's word and promises become our power, truth, and wisdom in our everyday life. Our actions, words, and deeds become Christlike because we confess and believe that He is the way, the truth, and life. We grow and flourish in faith, rooted and grounded in Jesus Christ, our Savior and Lord.

Thanks be to God.

Amen.

BLIND, BUT NOW I SEE

The Lord opens the eyes of the blind. The Lord lifts up those who are bowed down, the Lord loves the righteous. (Psalm 146:8)

Then the eyes of the blind shall be opened, and the ears of the deaf unstopped. (Isaiah 35:5)

Having the eyes of your hearts enlightened that you may know what is the hope to which He has called you, what are the riches of his glorious inheritance in the saints. (Ephesians 1:18)

Life is like a merry-go-round or a carousel. The ups and downs of life is never-ending.

We all go round and round in our own circle of life. We stay in our own safe and predictable world. We become blind to the things happening around us. We are not physically blind, but we become blinded by our own selfishness and unwillingness to see others, to help them, and address their needs.

As a child of God, He calls each of us to live differently, to live for Him, not ourselves.

He wants us to show others His love and to help them as Jesus helps us. When we ask Jesus to forgive our sins and our blindness, He opens our eyes and heart. His forgiving love extends to every part of our being. He spreads His love throughout our heart, He fills our mind with more Christ like behaviors, and He floods our soul with His humility, righteousness, and wisdom to help others.

Our relationship with Jesus deepens; and the eyes of our heart, soul, and mind open to the wonders and glories of His love to be of service and blessing to others for His name's sake. I was blind, but now I see because of Jesus Christ.

Thanks be to God. Amen.

CONVENIENT OR COMMITMENT

All scripture is inspired by God and profitable for teaching, for reproof, for correction and for training in Righteousness. (2 Timothy 3:16)

Commit your way to the Lord; trust in Him, and He will act. (Psalm 37:5)

And when they had appointed elder for them in every church, with prayer and fasting, they committed them to the Lord in whom they believed. (Acts 14:23)

A convenience store is part of our current society's one-stop shopping, everything in one place. It is just a quick stop for gas, snacks, or money—all conveniently located in one place. So one is able to be on his way quickly and conveniently.

Some of us try to put God in the same category—convenient or a drive-through. God has everything we need sitting on a shelf. All we need to do is stop, pick up what we need, and then on our way, without a second thought, coming and going as we please.

However, God is not a convenience store. His love for us is not, nor was it ever, convenient or easy. What Jesus does for us is not convenient or quick or easy. Jesus did not die on the cross to forgive our sins for it to be convenient. We cannot just pick up what we need off a shelf in His store and be on our way. It does not work that way.

When we believe and trust in Him, we become His children. We commit our lives to Him. He provides and satisfies us with His love, mercy, and forgiveness. We devote our time and effort in reading and studying His word and growing in faith and trust in Him and His love. It is a commitment and a way of life. It is not "come and go as you please."

Our ministry and serving a Risen Lord is not convenient, it is a commitment we make. It is because of His love for us and because of the cross we are free from sin and death. It is a life-changing experience. It is renewal of our heart, mind, and soul. We commit our heart, mind, and soul to the Lord, and He promises to always be with us, to help, and to protect us. His steadfast love and faithfulness to His children is everlasting.

Our hope is in the Lord, and He does not disappoint those who commit their way unto Him.

Thanks be to God.

Amen.

Faith in Action

He has showed you, O man, what is good; and what does the Lord require of you, but to do justice, and to love kindness, and to walk humbly with God? (Micah 6:8)

As each has received a gift, employ it for one another, as good stewards of God's varied grace. (1 Peter 4:10)

God is able to provide you with every blessing in abundance so you may always have enough of everything and may provide in abundance for every good work. (1 Corinthians 4:10)

Faith in action is when we live for Christ, not ourselves. It is each of us doing the ministry He calls us to do, out of our love for Him. Since everything we have comes from the Lord, our faith in actions means being a good caretaker of all that He gives and entrusts to us; this includes His word, the Gospel. It is also our whole life in service to Him, who is our Lord and Savior.

When we believe and trust in Jesus, we become part of the family of God. And being part of the family includes forgiving and loving others as God forgives and loves us. It involves giving, sharing, and serving others in our home, in our family, our community, and in the workplace. And in so doing, we seek Him for His help and ask Him to provide for us and supply all our needs for our serving and ministry. He is able to transform our selfish hearts and minds to be caring, loving, and generous to others. As we believe, trust, and walk with God, we show and reflect to others God's love and truth through our words, actions, and deeds. He blesses us with all we have and with all good things to be a blessing to others. This is our faith in action.

Thanks be to God.

Amen.

GROW IN GOD'S GRACE AND LOVE

Jesus is the answer. He helps us grow in faith, gives us strength and endurance and peace for our journey. He never runs out of love, peace, comfort, strength, endurance, or anything we need. Seek Him and ask in His name.

Therefore, we should never give up on Him and His love for us. We should never give up on ourselves, our hopes, and dreams because with God, all things are possible and every day is a new day. Allow Jesus into your life. Let His love abound and faith increase. Cling to Him and never grow weary in serving God, sharing His Gospel and showing love to others. Let us be the face of Jesus to all.

Lord, help us all to know You and realize Your great love for each of us. Thank You for sending Your Son to save us. Thank You for supplying all our needs every day. And when we lose our way, guide and direct us back to You. Help us to use our life, our gifts, and our blessings to grow in grace and in love. Help us to give of ourselves, to be a light and blessing to others.

> The Lord bless you and keep you; the Lord make His face to shine upon you, and be gracious to you: The Lord lift up His countenance upon you, and give you peace. (Numbers 6:24–26)

Thanks be to God.
Amen.

About the Author

Kathy Tuff Fleiger grew up in Alaska and Minnesota and then moved to Spokane, Washington, where she currently lives. She is a wife, mother, and grandmother.

She is a retired physical therapist who worked with children with physical disabilities.

Kathy was raised in the church and continues to be active in the church. She has taught the Bethel Bible Series as well as high school and adult Sunday school classes.

Writing is another way God has called Kathy to share her insights and talks with Him about His word and everlasting love to others. When Kathy is not writing, she enjoys spending time with her wonderful and supportive husband, grandchildren, children and their spouses, sisters, and brother. She also loves the active outdoor lifestyle of the Pacific Northwest, which includes golfing, kayaking, and hiking.

CPSIA information can be obtained
at www.ICGtesting.com
Printed in the USA
LVHW030805040420
652211LV00002B/248